For people having gone through a pandemic (with deep, unsettling effects), this book offers an intelligent, traditional, and yet not predictable account of five basic Christian beliefs that can help us, not to return to a previous Christian comfort zone, but to rediscover old truths as if for the first time. The author starts with the belief in God as Creator which, he says, is the beginning of an adventure. The second basic Christian claim is sin, which, oddly, is not something substantial but rather a hole in reality. Third is that God is active in the mess of things; fourth, that God has shown, in Jesus, what a real human being is. Finally, this adventure is throughout an ongoing discovery that in Jesus Christ people have their true friend.

At the end of each chapter are open-ended discussion questions, making this volume easily used for group study.

This book is especially for

- *people who are thinking again about fundamentals of Christian faith and whether they should reconsider them*

- *Christians who have felt their faith weakened or damaged, or who have felt questions raised during the pandemic that challenge what they thought Christianity believed*

- *Church leaders looking for resources and encouragement to take up deeper formation in Christian faith as part of the process of reemergence*

A Post-COVID
Catechesis

A Post-COVID Catechesis

VICTOR LEE AUSTIN

CASCADE *Books* • Eugene, Oregon

Cascade Books
An Imprint of Wipf and Stock Publishers
199 W. 8th Ave., Suite 3
Eugene, OR 97401

www.wipfandstock.com

PAPERBACK ISBN: 978-1-6667-3041-8
HARDCOVER ISBN: 978-1-6667-2193-5
EBOOK ISBN: 978-1-6667-2194-2

Cataloguing-in-Publication data:

Names: Austin, Victor Lee.

Title: A Post-COVID Catechesis / Victor Lee Austin.

Description: Eugene, OR : Cascade Books, 2022 | Includes bibliographical references.

Identifiers: ISBN 978-1-6667-3041-8 (paperback) | ISBN 978-1-6667-2193-5 (hardcover) | ISBN 978-1-6667-2194-2 (ebook)

Subjects: LCSH: Diseases—Religious aspects—Christianity. | COVID-19 (Disease)—Religious aspects—Christianity.

Classification: BV4637 .A98 2022 (paperback) | BV4637 .A98 (ebook)

03/21/22

To uncounted teachers and students,
disciples all,
and in honor of
George R. Sumner,
Brian Davies,
and
Andrew C. Mead,
teachers of the faith

Contents

Introduction

The shutdown of churches during the time of the pandemic cost us seriously. Online worship services, even for those who joined them regularly over whatever platform, provoked memory of that which had been and was no longer. As a friend said (to explain why he no longer tuned into church online), "Facebook Live just doesn't do it for me." Broadcast worship and teaching were not new, of course, nor was an awareness of their inadequacy. A generation ago, some mainline Protestant ads took aim at televangelists and their kin: a picture of a TV, a white cloth draped over it, cup and plate upon the cloth, and above it all, words like these: "When was the last time your TV set gave you communion?"

Even when churches were permitted to reopen, the experience was constrained. Concern over possible transmission of the virus required that worshipers stay at a distance from each another. Silenced was almost all participatory singing; hidden behind masks was that most beautiful of God's creations, the human face; novel procedures for separating people were implemented; and much more. Yet even this altered, limited, constrained worshiping was welcome—and the blow thus harder when, no sooner than people got used to it, it was taken away, as, sadly, churches staying open was deemed no longer safe.

For more than a year, social events hardly happened. A novel term, *social distancing*, entered the jargon of disease control and became ubiquitous, with the imperative verb *practice* attached to it. We human beings were instructed night and day, at every turn, to learn to practice something that is inherently unhuman. That is to say, social beings (which we humans are) were being told to get used to being unsocial.[1]

Education went online and, for adults, was perhaps less affected by the pandemic than some other activities. But one missed the give-and-take of having people in the same room. As a sometime teacher, I found myself noticing the absence of opportunities for informal conversation that used to await us in church or school hallways. Furthermore, and most fundamentally, deep, transformative learning occurs dialectically. Student and teacher alike need to question, to weigh, to listen, to respond. This is true especially when the subject is theology. God's word does not enter our brains the way grain enters a grain elevator. The word grows in our heart, nourished by our encounters with one another. Online, those encounters are two-dimensional. They are as flat as our screens.

Reality, of course, prevails in the long run, which on this matter became evident just a few months into lockdown. People tired of educational platforms like Zoom. One heard people say they were "Zoomed out." I know I was. And I (along with you, dear reader, in all likelihood) am part of the lucky crowd of people who enjoy reading; we are part of what sociologists call the knowledge class. Getting through COVID was easier for the likes of us than for most everyone else. Perhaps the greatest and still-incalculable harms were done to children denied in-person learning.

I have heard it said that, when the church acquiesced in shutting down, it lost significant credibility, both with its own members and in the wider culture. I do not know if this is the case "significantly," but it does seem to have been a missed opportunity: to push back and proclaim that we in the church have something essential

---

1. At the end of 2020, I heard it said in a church in Arizona: Please practice "physical distancing." Later I heard the same phrase over the airport intercom. Physical distancing is, of course, precisely what the public health directive was trying to encourage. That it was euphemistically called "social" (as if "social" were a gentler adjective than the outright "physical"), despite the underlying threat that "social distancing" poses to our inherent humanity, could well have been a product of blind spots in the public health response to the disease: the lack of collaborative input and buy-in from sociologists, anthropologists, group psychologists, even philosophers and theologians. Concerning this lack, an interesting historical analogue is given by Taylor Dotson, "Radiation Politics."

that human communities need, *especially* in times of pandemic. On the face of it, the message conveyed by acquiescence in shutdown is that we have nothing to offer that is essential to human life.

Reports of church overseers (not, may I hasten to add, my bishop) telling their clergy that "our number one priority is safety" seemed to reveal a lack of belief in, for one thing, the resurrection.[2] The Gospels do not endorse a "safety is number one" ecclesiastical message; to the contrary, they undermine it. The Gospels say: do not fear death! Thus the emphasis on safety was at odds with having a coherent evangelical message. Nor did the churches' acquiescence in exclusion from the bedside of dying people manifest a belief that we have anything important to offer at that time. The traditional, so-called last rites that include anointing, laying on of hands, prayer, and holy communion were revealed to be things we could give up without audible protest—as if Episcopalians (to pick on my own tribe) no longer much believe the words they say.[3]

2. Similarly, any organization that says their number one priority is safety reveals a lack of belief in their own reason for being. If an airline company proclaims their number one priority is safety, they should just shut down. There is always risk in getting on an airplane (not to mention the risk of getting to and from an airport). What they mean (but don't say) is, given our number one priority (which is to be the best airplane company around), we are doing all we can to carry out that priority safely.

There is no enterprise, no human activity, ever, whose overriding goal is safety. Safety is *by definition* subordinate to other purposes.

3 Following one of the early reopening services, when we clergy were masked and greeted people at a distance, one woman told me of her serious illness. I asked her if I might lay my hand on her head and pray. She said yes, and so we did. A few months later, she told me I was the only person to do so.

I mention this not because I am brave or unique—I am sure many other clergy did similar things that bespoke similar trust in the Lord and evoked similar gratitude—but because I saw in her the need we all have, when we are faced with overwhelming situations, for prayer and touch. In the extended conclusion of Saint Mark, believers are called to "lay hands on the sick" (16:18), even as Paul did to "the father of Publius" who "lay sick of a fever and of a bloody flux"; Paul "entered in, and prayed, and laid his hands on him" (Acts 28:8). Oliver O'Donovan considers the "laying-on of hands," in all its various uses, to be "the sign of the church's empowerment"; it is "one sign, used in different contexts but with a single thread of meaning," by which we call "for the invasion of God's power to break the fetters of impotence" (O'Donovan, *Desire of the Nations*, 190).

Friends from other denominations, both Roman Catholic and Protestant, tell me similar stories from their contexts.

It is important to acknowledge, to take the time to give voice to, these unhappy reflections, although of course there are responses. For one thing, churches did not merely acquiesce to COVID restrictions, but they tried to be the church in new ways, especially online. Many of my fellow clergy were working harder than ever, innovating with technological tools, pushing out content onto the web, staying in touch with their people. Nonetheless, the faithfulness question refuses to disappear. We worked hard, but were we faithful to the gospel? The church has been unfaithful before; and as we come to grips with what has happened, I expect we will come to see patterns of unfaithfulness in the COVID period as well.

But such judgments are for the future, not for the book at hand. To repeat, I do not know if this sense of a loss of credibility is widespread in our churches or in our culture. Indeed, the culture may not have even noticed what the church was doing. It is clear that Christianity is a sideline in America today, and even if it is no more sideline now than pre-COVID, it remains undeniably so. Which is to say, we may not have lost much credibility during CO-VID because we had so little to start with.

What then is our task now? What does Christian mission require now?

It requires a sober acceptance of the costs of the pandemic period. For regardless of why they happened—the lockdowns; the tentative, constricted, and extended months of partial reopenings—the church is in a new and weakened situation. In the post-COVID period, we doubtless need to think again about methods of evangelism and the place of technology, not to mention other significant matters of church functioning.

Most deeply, we need an intentional return to the basics of Christian belief. There are two reasons for this. First, churches need to demonstrate their fidelity to Christian truth, which they can do by setting it forth with clarity and conviction. This is a matter of claiming our core identity as apostolic. Second, every human being needs to hear that truth now. This is a matter of hearing the good if complicated news of what, in God's creative and redemptive eyes, a human being is.

Our need is for rock-solid teaching that bears down on the core of Christian belief and sets forth that belief appropriately to the post-pandemic period. We need to speak of the triune God in ways that illuminate the glories of human beings. We need to give an account of reality that draws us to high things, far beyond the confinements of safety. And we need to do all this in close connection with the Bible, while using words that speak to ordinary human intelligence.

Such convictions have spurred me to venture this catechism. It is not a comprehensive document. It hardly touches on vast regions of Christian theology; it has little to say about techniques of prayer; it is not much interested in giving an account of sacraments and worship. This catechism is, deliberately, limited to five topics that I believe need our focused attention as we seek to join with God in rebuilding Christian faith in our new situation. These are topics that those who have returned to our churches after a year or more of online worship need to understand. And they are topics of relevance to those who are not Christian today. We have a story of God and humanity that is lofty and challenging and worth giving your life for.

These five topics fit into a story that begins with creation. God is the solid ground, the Guarantor of all that is. We then turn to sin (chapter 2) and to God's Speech and God's Spirit, active in the midst and the mess of things (chapter 3). Finally we devote two chapters to Jesus Christ, one on his life and teaching ("Behold the human being!"—chapter 4) and one on his death and resurrection ("Behold our true friend!"—chapter 5).

Let's go.

CHAPTER 1

Creation

The adventure that begins when we believe in God as Creator—the question of God as the Creator of SARS-CoV-2—the illusion and temptation of safety

To believe in God is to begin an adventure.

The reason is, God is not any person, real or fictional. To believe in God is to believe in neither an imaginary person nor an actual. God is not Santa Claus. God is not Thor or Zeus or Athena; nor is he Jeff Bezos, nor Ruth Bader Ginsburg, nor Aunt Sally, nor Gandalf, nor James Earl Jones (although, illogical as it is, I like to think he has the voice of James Earl Jones). Nor is God that boy who can bend spoons with his mind in the Matrix. God is not a Mark Zuckerberg who, if only you could get through to him, could give you a hundred grand (spare change to him, life-changing to you). God is not a Joe Biden who, if only you got through to him, might pardon you for your crimes and misdeeds.

God is not a powerful wind that could blow the windows out of your house.

God is not a sweet thought that can calm an anxious dream.

God is nothing in the world. In fact, if by *something* we mean a constituent of the universe, a being in space or time or both, a thing that can be put alongside other things, then God is not something.

God is nothing in the world *because God is the Creator of the world.*

The Creator is the reason the creation exists. To believe in God is to recognize that things are not self-explanatory. Your own life: say all you can say about it—where you grew up, how your parents reared you, what you did with your friends, your whole life story—there always remains something else that needs to be said. None of us is the entire explanation for ourselves. There is always something more.

And that is true of the universe as a whole. The universe cannot explain itself. Yes, parts of the universe can explain other parts, but the whole cannot explain the whole. Having learned much from theologian Herbert McCabe, I like to put this question as: how come the whole shebang anyway?[1]

Or as the epigrammatic philosopher Ludwig Wittgenstein put it: the mystery is not *how* the world is but *that* the world is.

To believe God is the Creator is to believe God is the reason for the whole shebang, the mystery that surrounds all existence. God, who is no thing in all creation, is the something more that is needed to understand any created thing.

Why do I call this the beginning of an adventure? It's because although the universe points to God its Creator, the universe cannot show God to us. The universe is God's creation, just as a novel is a writer's creation or a song is a musician's creation. When you're reading a novel, you don't expect to find the author popping up on a page. Harry Potter doesn't suddenly start talking with J. K. Rowling. And if he did, of course, the J. K. Rowling to whom he was talking would be a character in the novel and not really the author herself. Autobiographies, too, inevitably fall short in this way: the person in the book is not really and completely the person writing the story.

---

1. See especially chapter 1 of McCabe, *God Matters*, where the reader will find also the following line from Wittgenstein, as well as McCabe's pithy formulations mentioned below.

Although there might be hints of the authorship of God in the world he has authored, you and I will never run into God the way we might run into Mark Zuckerberg.

I emphasize this because a lot of people misunderstand Christianity. They think that when we talk about God we are talking about a person like Mark Zuckerberg, only bigger and better. (I mean no disrespect to Mr. Zuckerberg; put any name there you want.) God, after all, looks like a proper noun, a word that names someone. So it seems that, just as *Mark Zuckerberg* names that Facebook guy, so *God* names that in-the-sky guy.

No.

God names the Creator, and the Creator is not someone to whom we can point. We cannot put God in a lineup. You'll never be in a room where, sitting in the various chairs, are your grandfather, Donald Trump, Cher, Lady Gaga, and God. In fact, you can't put any creatures and their Creator within the same frame. And you can't put the creation itself, the whole shebang, in the same frame with the Creator.

Another great line from Herbert McCabe: God plus the universe do not make two.

Here we find our adventure. We realize God is real and we believe in him, but at the same time we realize God is not like anything in our experience. God doesn't even fit into our normal language.

Super-elusive, this God. To believe in him gets wilder and more wonderful with every step.

So how do we know about this God? First, we can know that God exists just through our realization that things don't make sense on their own. We need a further explanation—even though that further explanation can be neither caught in our own reason nor put into words that are adequate.

But because it is hard for humans to get this point on their own, God has revealed it to us. The Ten Commandments begin with the affirmation "I am the LORD thy God" (Deut 5:6). In the

Psalms, the poet says: "As for all the gods of the nations, they are but idols; but it is the LORD who made the heavens" (Ps 96:5).[2] When the Bible says "idols," it means created beings or things that are purported to be gods but that really aren't. The reason all idols are false gods is that they are, in the end, creatures with confused pretensions. An idol might be the figment of someone's imagination; it might be a spiritual being that presumed upon usurping its Creator; but, whatever it is, an idol is a thing, a creation. In the great Creator/creature divide, idols fall on the side of creatures. Idols are not gods.

There cannot be two gods, because to be God is to be the Creator, and there can't be two creators.

Nonetheless, there is a possible misunderstanding when we say there is one God. If I say I have one cat (which I don't; this is just a bad dream), you would understand me as saying that while I could have been so foolish as to have two or three or a hundred cats, I have been a very restrained person (if still foolish) and have limited myself to a single feline companion. If I say I had one hamburger last week, similarly you would understand me to be saying that I risked heart attack and perhaps participated in the evil of industrial cattle-raising in order to enjoy one of the high pleasures of American life but that, with admirable restraint, I did it only once.

But if I say "I believe in one God," it does not mean that, although I could have chosen to do otherwise, I have chastely and wisely limited my worship to a single divine being. No. God is not a countable entity. There is no difference between saying "I believe in God" and "I believe in one God" (as the Apostles' and Nicene creeds have it, respectively).

That God is not countable is still another way of saying that God plus the creation do not make two.

---

2. All quotations from the Psalms are from, and follow the numbering of, the 1979 Book of Common Prayer of the Episcopal Church. Unless otherwise noted, all other biblical quotations are from the Authorized Version, commonly called the King James Version.

Our adventure continues when we come upon the following truth: God did not have to create. In fact, God doesn't have to do anything. We say this not because we understand it, but because the opposite must be false. It makes no sense to say God could be under some constraint that would make him do something. If there is something that makes God act, then that something would be the real God, and what we were thinking of as God would be its creature.

This is what is meant when people say creation is "gratuitous." Another marvelous twentieth-century theologian, Robert Farrar Capon, says the whole universe is like an "orange peeling hung on God's chandelier."[3] It doesn't have to be there, but, inexplicably to us, God seems rather to like it—and so it stays.

Which is to say, there is no reason for you and me to continue in existence for another second, no reason for the whole shebang to go on from moment to moment, no reason for that orange peel to keep on hanging there. God's creation is not so much a beginning of the universe as it is a holding of the universe in being. Yes, God created you (he seems to have done so at that wonderful moment when a lucky sperm cell won the race to the egg). But God also creates you every second.

Take a breath.

He just did it again.

That the whole shebang keeps on going is a sign that God likes it. And here our adventure in believing in God the Creator takes a turn back to the creation itself. As God seems to like the whole shebang (that orange peeling hung on the chandelier), so we are set a task of learning to find the world likeable.

Try this on for size:

If it exists, it's beautiful.

I'm sure God finds sunsets beautiful (although I have no idea what it means for God to look at a sunset). But does God find trash beautiful?

Well, trash exists, doesn't it?

3. Capon, *Supper of the Lamb*, 5.

It strikes me that part of the adventure of faith is to find beauty in things that don't immediately strike me as beautiful. Have you ever lived in a house with a child who is learning to play a violin? The sound produced is painfully screeching; it's like fingernails on a chalkboard. But it's also a necessary phase, part of the birth pangs of a string musician. Listen carefully and you may find you are hearing, along with the teeth-grinding screeches, some amazingly lovely tones of growth.

Or an example that's more, well, tangible: have you ever changed a diaper? It's smelly, and it's a situation where disease might be transmitted; one needs to do it right. But it's also a way of showing love, of caring for another person.

Trash can be beautiful in that sense: like unmusical beginnings or like a dirty diaper, it is what we slough off as we go through life, and, as such, it has a certain beauty. The way we handle trash can be a sign of how we care for one another.

Of course, a lot of trash in our world has been needlessly trashed. It might instead have been recycled or reused, or it might never have become trash in the first place. Nonetheless, even the discards of a throwaway society can themselves be beautiful things. We might say, what a shame that toy wasn't kept or shared! But in saying that, we are seeing that it is still a good and interesting toy.

There are, you see, moral consequences to believing in God as Creator. We start trying to like the world, and that can lead us to change how we treat the world.

The Bible tells us that after the flood (Gen 6–8), God promised never to do it again, never again to do that all-encompassing flooding, never again to try to blot out the whole shebang and start over. Although nothing forced his hand, God decided to commit himself to the creation to the extent that, come what may, he will not wipe creation out.

No matter how stinky that orange peeling gets, God is going to keep it around.

Try this on for size:

If it's real, it's good.

This one doesn't seem right, does it? Hurricanes hit the coast and cause death, illness, wreckage, moldy conditions, homelessness, and more. They are very real, and they don't seem good. What good is a hurricane?

But that question, posed with understandable skepticism, does seem to have an answer. Hurricanes are a feature of the earth having the atmosphere that it has. I'm no meteorologist, but I'd guess that to get rid of hurricanes we'd have to stop the earth's rotation; and if it didn't rotate, it wouldn't be the fertile planet that it is. Hurricanes and tornadoes, and in a different sense earthquakes and tsunamis, are what you get when you get the earth.

Thinking about hurricanes can take us from an initial sense of their badness to a place of humility about our ability to judge badness. Although they don't seem good to us when and where they happen (indeed, their human consequences can be horrific), hurricanes are nonetheless a feature of a good, rotating, life-supporting earth. We call them bad because they can hurt us. But in the big picture, they have their place.

So try this on for size:

Even dangerous reality is good.

Goodness, it seems, is not human-centric. When God likes that orange peel, it's not because it guarantees a life free of danger for human beings. He likes thunderstorms as much as calm sunny beaches. They are all real, and beautiful, and good.

I know a priest who would write: "God damn COVID!" He meant it literally as a request for God to damn the disease. I approve of the strong feeling, borne from the enormity of the harm the virus has done to humanity. And it's not just to humanity in the abstract, it's our friends and neighbors who have died from it; it's personal. I also approve of the urgent request that God bring evil things to damnation—which I would take to be, to nonexistence. "Send the virus to hell!" is pretty much the same as "Send the virus to nonexistence!"

But despite all this, is it true that the virus itself is a bad thing? Bad for us, undeniably; bad for the planet as a whole, possibly. But bad in itself?

Like me, you have probably seen pictures of it. It is a visually beautiful particle, an individual of this virus, this "severe acute respiratory syndrome coronavirus 2," when enlarged to a size that we are able to see it. A poet might even call it regal, playing on the "corona" in its name. Also awesome is its canny power to co-opt a host cell and cause it to multiply copies of the virus, an undertaking of awesomely intricate complexity. Molecular biologists who study it learn about an incredible yet tiny thing. Indeed, that we can know about it anything at all induces amazement.

If it weren't killing us, we'd gladly acknowledge all this beauty.

All viruses are awesome and mysterious, and yet so tiny. I am told that if we queued up a hundred thousand virus particles in a straight line, it would still be shorter than an inch. (Okay, for big fat viruses, maybe two inches; but for little skinny ones, merely a tenth of an inch.) Yet what are they? Metaphysically, they are exceedingly strange. Viruses exist on the borderline between living things and inanimate matter, neither themselves alive nor yet exactly dead, either: they have DNA or RNA (SARS-CoV-2 has RNA) yet they cannot reproduce on their own (as, for instance, a cell can, by dividing). Scientific articles won't call an individual virus a *cell* or any other word a layperson might expect; they will use something neutral, like *particle*, because viruses don't fit in.

Viruses are like evening and morning, neither light nor dark, neither day nor night, and yet they are there. Talk about believing in God as starting an adventure! I think there's a hint of this in Genesis: "God divided the light from the darkness. . . . And the evening and the morning were the first day" (1:4–5). It is a hint that no matter how straightforward creation seems, there is still more there.

Creation is not self-explanatory, and amazing borderline things like virus particles are yet another way that it points us to the mystery that is beyond creation.

Strange wonder like this attaches also to many molecules, to other viruses, to bacteria, and so forth. Creation is staggeringly awesome, as Pascal grasped, not only in the infinite vastness of the heavens but also in the infinitesimal vastness within the microscopic world.

If we never had to think about its effect upon us, if we could just consider it in itself, I think we would unhesitatingly say that SARS-CoV-2 is real and beautiful and good. Nonetheless, as I write this, multiple millions of people have already died from it. Every reader of this book will know, or know of, some of them. And the fatalities around the world continue to grow. Can something so awful really be good?

When Job is grievously tormented by disease and the loss of his children and his possessions, he refuses to take a simple answer. In fact, from the beginning of his troubles to the end of his book, there is no answer in words that satisfies him. Yet, in the end, he is satisfied. What satisfies him is not an answer but a walk with God on creation's wild side.

God wants Job to see how the universe contains awesome and beautiful things that exist independently of human beings and, in fact, have no care for humans, don't know about humans, and are beyond the capacity of humans to control. Let us consider one of the beasts that Job sees when he walks on the wild side, that Leviathan, the final creature that God asks Job about (see Job 41).

Leviathan lives in the sea. No one could catch him with a fishing line. No one could force a hook into his nose. He would not plead with Job for mercy; he would not make a covenant with Job; he will never sport about with Job. Job cannot cook him and serve him up in a banquet for his friends. Job cannot even put a barbed wire into his skin. In fact, if Job were to touch him, Leviathan would kill Job instantly, and Job would remember no more.

This is not the last thing that God says to Job, but already we get the point. Leviathan is covered with a hide of scales such that nothing can harm him, and he can destroy any other creature that might come in his way—and he would do the destruction without even thinking about it.

Let it sink in.

God has made a creature that can have no interactions, no fellowship, with human beings. Nonetheless, this creature in his own way is real and good and beautiful—awesome in his power, his strength, his movements, his firm and hard heart, his impenetrable skin.

The penny drops: Job's affliction was in his skin. Job sees that he and Leviathan are completely different. From a walk on the wild side, Job learns—God brings him to appreciate—that the universe contains things he can never live alongside. And simultaneously with this insight, Job becomes grateful that God has made a place within the universe where a vulnerable man can live with other vulnerable men and women. The place God has made for Job is not a safe place, but it is a human place, a place of kin and neighbors and friends.

At the end of the first part of Walter Miller's post-nuclear-apocalypse novel, set in a largely lawless future, a monk is returning from New Rome (somewhere in the former American Midwest) when he is attacked by bandits, misshapen products of then-ancient radiation. They kill him instantly and set about to eat him. Buzzards feed on what is left. A mysterious wanderer espies the circling buzzards from a distance and reckons there is meat to be had there. He approaches, and when he finds it is the corpse of a man, albeit with many parts now missing, he knows what he has to do. He digs, and he buries. The author's point of view then shifts to the buzzards. Unable to finish eating this man, they fly off and are happy to find a dead hog. They glide down to enjoy a feast. Later, they find the remains of a cougar's meal.

And then, as if we were reading a late chapter in the book of Job, we are told: "The buzzards laid their eggs in season and lovingly fed their young." And then: "The younger generation waxed strong, soared high and far on black wings, waiting for the fruitful Earth to yield up her bountiful carrion." The buzzards multiply and fly farther afield, continuing to lay their eggs and feed their young. "Earth had nourished them bountifully for centuries. She would nourish them for centuries more."

The tragic end to that monk's life, it seems, is not tragic from every point of view. For the buzzards, it was part of God's providence, an aspect of how the earth, which he had created, provided for their needs.[4]

To believe in God is to begin an adventure that not only asks us to try to see creation as beautiful but also challenges us not to see ourselves as the center of all things. The creation that God likes, that nothing forced him to create, that he could stop holding in being any time he wanted (but has promised through Noah he will not), is nonetheless not a safe creation.

To believe in God is to embark on a journey that takes us out of safety.

To walk with God is sometimes to walk on the wild side, a place where Leviathan dwells, a place where viruses lurk.

Why anybody who reads the Bible would ever think the point of having faith is to secure a safe life is utterly beyond comprehension!

Safety?

Tell that to Jonah, swallowed within the belly of the fish or, later, scorching in the heat of the desert sun.

Tell that to Job, impoverished and covered with sores.

Tell that to the disciples, as their teacher expires on the crossbeam.

Creation is vast and awesome and fascinating. But it is not safe. God makes a world that has lots of things in it, and huge expanses of space, with which and in which no human being could live.

4. Miller, *Canticle for Leibowitz*. All quotations above are from p. 118.

Still we want to ask: why did God allow the virus SARS-CoV-2 to appear?

It seems hard to voice the answer that I am going to voice, hard because of the vast harm the virus has brought to human life all over the world, the deaths, the hospitalizations, the isolation in fear of catching it, the depression that follows upon human isolation, the shutdown of almost all communal activities, the uncounted economic loss that will have to be paid by the next generation, yea, even by the children who have been deprived of communal instruction and formation for, in some places, a full year and more. The toll of the virus cannot yet be measured; nonetheless, it is certain to be immense. How can such a thing be good? How can God allow such a thing?

Dear reader, you already have the tools to answer this. It is good because it exists, just as Leviathan is good and buzzards are good. The virus performs its activities with amazing cleverness on a microscopic level. And so on.

All this can be said on the assumption that the virus appeared as a result of normal or natural mutation in a sort of being that is naturally highly subject to mutation. Cold viruses and the flu are that way also. These changes, however harmful to human beings, are strictly analogous to earthquakes and hurricanes and the like. The harm they bring to humans is just the sort of risk humans have for being in the creation at all.

But there are aspects of the virus that would take us into a new theological category, namely, the category of sin. (Yet it is not precisely new, having been in the shadows all along; we glanced briefly upon sin, for instance, when we thought about trash that should not have been trashed.) If there were a deliberate human cause in the development of the virus or a culpable carelessness in a laboratory, we are talking not only about creation but about creation and sin. If the virus developed as a consequence of human harm to the environment, that also would be a matter of sin. And if authorities, in the response to the virus, hid information or misled people or overstated the clarity of what came to be called "the science" (note the definite article), then those, too, were occasions of sin.

Readers will have differing views on these questions, which is as it should be. The evidence, as I write, is only circumstantial and under renewed investigation. A clear understanding of the origins of the virus and the human causes of its spread may never be attainable.

But sin is likely to be a part of this picture, as it is a part of most human pictures. So as this pandemic recedes into our past, the post-pandemic theology we need is not only that of creation but also of sin.

To which we now turn.

DISCUSSION QUESTIONS FOR CHAPTER 1

1. The author goes on at some length about the belief in God as Creator, meaning that God is nothing in the world. What do you find interesting about that argument? What questions does it raise for you?

2. One claim in this chapter is that if we grasp that the world is a creation, we will see that God must like it somehow. The author says that this insight becomes a moral claim upon us, that we should learn to see everything that exists as, in some way, beautiful and good. Does this argument make sense to you? What would it mean for you to try to see beauty in everything that exists?

3. When Lady Gaga sings a song, is God the cause of her singing? Why or why not?

4. Job is invoked in this chapter as someone who experienced the vulnerability, the lack of safety, of human life in this world. What thoughts do you have about why God does not guarantee us a safe life?

CHAPTER 2

Sin

A human mystery, a nothing where there ought to be something—there is no adequate explanation—"What were they thinking!"—how did we start sinning?—the social character of sin

If creation points to a mystery about God, sin points to a mystery about human beings. When we see the world as a creation, we recognize that it cannot explain itself. Thus to believe in God as the Creator is to embark upon the exploration of a mystery.

In a reverse-mirror sense, sin points to a human mystery that also cannot be explained. But in the case of sin, there is literally nothing else that can explain it. Sin is a hole in the universe, a stone in the place of a human heart, a nothing where there ought to be something.

In Shakespeare's *King Lear* (act 1, sc. 4), the fool asks, "Can you make no use of nothing, nuncle?" To which Lear replies, "Why, no, boy; nothing can be made out of nothing." Earlier, commanded to give voice to her love for her father, Lear's daughter Cordelia had replied with the word "Nothing," pointing to the wrongness of her father's demand. The fool's question speaks to Lear's sin of pride, his failure to recognize his daughter Cordelia's integrity; and for Lear's sin, as for all sin, there is no explanation. Nothing can explain nothing.

People typically think of sins as actions. At one point, the apostle Paul erupts with self-exasperation that he does not do what he wants to do, and the thing he does is the very thing he does not want to do. A liturgical prayer of confession of sin often expresses that Pauline helplessness in the face of our own deeds, for instance: "We have left undone those things which we ought to have done, and we have done those things which we ought not to have done."[1]

We think of sins as concrete events, things done or left undone, events in which we participated and for which we have responsibility, or events which we avoided and for which avoidance we also have responsibility. In this way of thinking, sins are culpable actions or inactions. All this, however, is only to scratch the surface of sin.

You are going out the door on the way to work, and you are speaking to your houseguest. You say, "Jack has soccer after school; could you pick him up at four?" But actually, soccer is tomorrow, and, today, Jack needs to be picked up at three. You were confused. You said something that was not true. Still, it is not a sin.

Aquinas has an example of a man enjoying sexual intercourse with a woman under the misapprehension that they are married. In fact, however, he was married to someone else. The act is adultery, but it is not a sin.[2] (Behind this hypothetical situation, it seems to me, might be the story of Jacob and Leah in Gen 29. Jacob thought he was married to Rachel, and he thought he was consummating that marriage. It was dark, however, and the girls' father had deceived Jacob. If he had been sleeping with Rachel, it would have been adultery, because he was, in fact, married to Leah—but he

---

1. Book of Common Prayer, 41–42; also 63.

2. Aquinas, *Summa Theologiae*, I-II.19.6. In Aquinas's analysis, the hypothetical situation involves an error of judgment about circumstantial fact; it is not (what would be morally culpable) an ignorance of the law against adultery. This non-culpable error of judgment renders the act involuntary, i.e., not, properly speaking, an act of the will. Roughly speaking, then, it is a mistake and not a sin.

would not have known it was adultery. Similarly, had he in fact been married to Rachel as he supposed he was, his actual sleeping with Leah would have been adultery—yet, again, he would not have known, since he thought he was with Rachel. The text does not indicate that Leah or Rachel had any agency in the matter.)

There is an important distinction to be made between mistakes and sin. Mistakes can be explained; sin cannot.

How can we know if an action is a sin? Discernment of sin seems exceedingly difficult, since any external description of an action might, in some situation, describe an action that is guiltless.

A man cuts off another man's leg, and he does so without the use of anesthesia. Normally this would be a form of torture and a grievous sin. But if the leg is gangrenous and no other medical care is at hand, it might be an action aimed at saving his life, a necessarily radical step towards healing.

Similarly, self-amputation is a sin in normal circumstances, but when a hiker who was trapped in an isolated place cut off his hand in order to free himself, it was a commendably heroic act. (The film *127 Hours* is based on this.)

In these and similar instances, we can give an account of the action that explains why it was done, and it is an account that is satisfactory. There was nothing else that could have been done, in the particular circumstances, that would have saved the life of the person involved.

What makes a sin is not what happens but what does not happen.

A woman robs her neighbor. The jewels she got are good things, beautiful in themselves and valuable on the market. Money itself is a good thing, worthy of our desiring it. There is nothing wrong with seeing the goodness, and thus desirability, of jewels and wealth and so on. The sin was that this woman desired those goods more than she desired to live in a friendly, loving way with her neighbor. She should have desired to love her neighbor more than she desired her neighbor's goods.

The good of one's neighbor is greater than the goods of one's neighbor.

Every sin is a desire for a good thing that is carried out at the expense of higher goods that ought to have been desired more. The highest good, humanly speaking, is to live with others as friends, which is what "loving your neighbor as yourself" amounts to. I think we can see this in the big sins rather easily. For instance, to pick up on an earlier example, sex is a good thing, but it is a sin when it is enjoyed at the cost of failing to love others (hence the prohibition of adultery).

The same is true even of run-of-the-mill sins. Obeying traffic laws is our way of loving our many neighbors who share the highway. If we dart between cars and aggressively tailgate others whose speed does not measure up to our desires, we endanger our neighbors. This is true even if the traffic laws fall short of being what they should be: to follow the laws is a small but significant way to show love for a neighbor.

If drivers customarily showed such consideration for one another, then in a situation where you had a passenger needing urgent medical care, you could drive aggressively fast. The rarity of that sort of driving would then be interpreted by other drivers as an indication you had an emergency at hand, and they would cheerfully move aside for you.

Aggressive drivers want to save time (arguably a good thing) or to enjoy the muscle power of their vehicle (also a good thing) or some other good. But they should desire more to love the other drivers.

The failure in sin is not what happens but what does not happen. That is to say, the failure in sin is the failure involved in choosing a lesser good when one should have chosen a higher good.

Precisely here is the mystery. There is no account that can be given that can explain this failure.

We can explain the thief's action: she wanted the jewels, she wanted the money to buy something, or whatever. But we can never explain why she wanted that more than she wanted to love her neighbor.

Have you ever looked at a situation and said, "What were they thinking?" It's a common saying. I noticed it once when someone was talking (this is not a political point; it happened a decade before the 2016 election) about the exceedingly smooth and slippery surface of the plaza in front of the Trump Tower on Fifth Avenue in New York City. It was a rainy day, and on the plaza there had been much slipping and sliding. She shook her head. "What were they thinking?"

Now I write that with a question mark, but my point is that it really isn't a question. We might learn that they were thinking that a certain marble had a lovely appearance. Or we might learn that that particular smooth stone was available at a good price. We might get a number of answers to our question. That is to say, we might be able to find out what in fact they were thinking.

But none of those answers would be adequate. For by those words, we really mean "What were they thinking!"—the exclamation point indicating that there is nothing that they might have been thinking that could explain the mess of the situation.

Sin has no explanation. If I look squarely at a sin I have committed, I am looking at a hole inside myself. Sin, personally examined, brings us to that vertiginous precipice where we catch a glimpse of a nothing that has been scooped out within us. This nothing is the opposite of the no thing that is the Creator who holds us in being; it is simply sheer absence. Look at your sins, and you won't see the metaphorical equivalents of bombs or rifle shots or slaps in the face or even the bystander who stayed in his chair rather than get up to see why a child was screaming. Look at your sins, and you won't see ugliness or cruelty.

You will see nothing.

Did God make us this way? No, because God creates everything that is. He does not create things that don't exist.

Sin is something that doesn't exist, in the precise sense of there being something that should exist but fails to be. Recall the thief: her desire for jewels is a good thing, a real thing, something about which we can give an account. Her failure to love her neighbor more than she loves her neighbor's jewels is her sin. Yet that sin is, to be precise, an absence, not a positive action but a failure of action. It is a hole in reality, something not there.

And if something is not there, it has not been created. Therefore God is not responsible for it. God did not make her a sinner.

On the other hand, God did, in fact, make human beings such that they—we—can fail to live up to our humanity. We are capable of falling short of our nature in a way that is, it seems, unique to our species. It is hard to think of a dog falling short of being a dog (perhaps it's less hard in the case of cats, but I'll let that pass). It is certainly hard to think of a virus falling short of being a virus. You'll never look at a mountain and say, "My, that mountain is doing a good job today of being a mountain!" But God made us such that it is a very common thing to say that we are doing a good job, or failing to do a good job, of being human.

What we say is: God made us capable of sin, but if we sin, since it is a failure of being fully ourselves, that failure is entirely ours.

All this is true only because of the exceedingly strange character of sin, it being a nothing. And it means, by the way, that there cannot be a person who is simply a sinner, full stop. No human being in the world is *nothing but* a sinner. No matter how awful the sin that has been committed is, as long as we still have a human being, we still have a being who is good and who is more than his or her sin.

You and I are more than our sins. And that is a comforting thought.

C. S. Lewis builds this truth into the landscape of his book *The Great Divorce*. The story opens with a fictional bus ride from Grey Town (which will be, in the end, Hell) to the outskirts of Heaven. Late in the story, the main character learns that when he came up from Grey Town, he didn't just cross space—he enlarged. All of that Grey Town, all of its thousands upon thousands of insubstantial, stretched-out miles, is contained in a bit of reality smaller than the tiniest piece of dirt there in the low plains of Heaven.

Sin causes the sinner to shrink, to become less real. In a memorable scene, the narrator witnesses the culmination of this transformation. A lovely woman (whom he first mistakes for the Virgin Mary but learns she was "just" an ordinary person who loved her neighbors) comes down from the heights of Heaven to meet the man who had been her husband, who has just come up on the bus from Grey Town. The man is so full of wounded pride that he cannot see anything outside himself. He gets smaller and smaller as they talk. And when he makes his final decision to say no to Love, he disappears.[3]

When sin overtakes us completely, we just go out of existence. Sin is a hole in reality; complete sinfulness would be a complete absence of reality.

If God did not create sin, how did it come about that we started sinning?

The scriptural account begins in Gen 2. There was an original human, created to till the soil. He is moved into a garden, where there is a tree from which he is not to eat: the tree of knowledge of good and bad. It is not good for this human to be alone, and the ultimate solution of his aloneness problem is the creation of woman out of his side. The subtlest of the creatures God made, before God made woman, takes it upon himself to insinuate to the woman certain ideas; as a result of their conversation, she decides to eat the fruit that was forbidden; she in turn gives some to the man, and he also eats.

This story is marvelously rich. One old interpretation is that the human sin was not the original sin in the cosmos, but, previously, some of the angels had rebelled against God. The book of Revelation tells of an event of angelic rebellion in which Michael was victorious and the devil cast down to the earth. The text identifies

3. Lewis, *Great Divorce*. See especially chs. 12–13.

the devil as an ancient deceiver and a serpent, details which would allow the serpent of Genesis 3 to be interpreted as the devil.

But this explanation—which may well be true—answers the question of the beginning of sin only by relocating it to an earlier place. For if we humans started sinning because Satan tempted us, we still haven't explained why his temptation was successful. On top of that, the explanation has added a new question: why did those angels sin? The question of why sin entered the cosmic picture remains unanswered, as sin remains inexplicable.

Another old interpretation is that sin is necessary in order for humans to grow. Just as the process of maturity in children requires that they make mistakes and learn from them, so the process of maturity of the human race requires sin, not for itself but for the opportunity it gives us of growing closer to God. After all, if a person never is tempted, then his or her goodness is unconscious. It is better to choose to be good than to be good without any thinking; however, in order to choose goodness, one must know what it is to choose badness.

A variation on this theory of the built-in necessity of sin is the claim, made by some old rabbis, that before humans sinned, the earth sinned. They note that in Genesis 1, on the third day of creation, God tells the earth to "grass grass,"[4] but the earth does not do that; it merely "puts forth" grass. On the sixth day, the tragic shortcoming of the earth is seen even more strongly. God commands that the "earth bring forth" the animals, but the earth does nothing; in the event, "God made" the animals (Gen 1:24–25).[5]

This view, in short, is that we are wrong to make a sharp distinction between sin and mistakes, that there are limitations built into things on account of which sin is inevitable. Sometimes,

---

4. To "grass grass" is Robert Sacks's translation of Gen 1:11: "And God said, 'Let the earth grass grass,'" his effort to render the grammatical construction of the cognate accusative. Sacks compares it to things like dancing a dance, where we find a unity between the object (a dance) and the action (a dancer). "The sentence, 'Let the earth grass grass,' is as strange in Hebrew as it is in English," he comments (Sacks, *Lion and Ass*, 6).

5. See Sacks, *Lion and Ass*, commentary on Gen 1:11 (pp. 6–8) and on 1:24–25 (pp. 15–16).

thinking along these lines, a theologian will claim that the fall was a "fall upwards."

This second line of interpretation, however, would require us to abandon the distinction between mistakes and sins. If we recognize that there are truly sins in the world—deeds that cannot be explained in terms of adequate accounts of the goods they aimed at—then it will not do to say sinning is based in the necessities of the world.

I want to say, furthermore, that it is not true that one has to sin in order to understand goodness. There are many examples in life where choosing a wrong thing makes it harder, subsequently, to choose a right thing. The first time you lie to your spouse, it might be very hard; but with repetition, it gets easier. One might eventually become a person who doesn't know the difference between a lie and the truth.

Conversely, surely the blessed ones in the life to come are perfectly free human beings. Yet, despite this complete freedom, they will never sin: their happiness and flourishing and eternal activities (whatever they are!) will continue and be joyful and interesting and creative without ever being diminished by jealousy or hate or envy or any other failure at being fully human. Sin is impossible in heaven; the people in heaven are perfectly free; therefore, it is possible for human beings to be free and flourishing without it being conceivable they would ever sin.

Which means, we still don't know why we started sinning.

Time for a summary.

Sin is a nothing of the following sort: every sinful act is a choice of a lesser good over a greater good. The failure to desire the good is a failure to be fully human; it is a step downwards; it is not something the Creator has brought about, because the Creator is responsible for the things that are, not the "things" that are not. (They, of course, really aren't things at all.) Why did the woman who stole her neighbor's gold not desire the love of her neighbor more than her neighbor's gold? It is not something explicable, because it is in reality a nothing. And the end of this process of choosing evil over good is to go out of existence.

I began chapter 1 with the claim that to believe in God is to launch into an adventure. Here is an unexpected discovery along the adventurous way: we cannot explain why there is sin in the world. Sin is absurd; there is no accounting for it. Nonetheless, it is real. Which leaves us with three things to consider.

First, that sin in itself is more than the mere accumulation of sins. There is more to sin than culpable action and inaction.

Second, the uncomfortable fact that even though sin makes no sense, we go on doing it.

Third, that God, not responsible for sin, is not happy with us failing to be fully human.

We will conclude this chapter with brief comments on the first two of these, and the third will launch us into the rest of the book.

There are clearly patterns of sin in the world. We give them names like lying and stealing. To have a word for something means that there is more than one instance of it. If there were only one cat in the world, and there never had been other cats, we would not call it a cat.

Lying is something that happens often enough for us to have a definition for the word. If Jose is lying to his wife, Gertrude, we know what sort of thing is going on, even if we are ignorant of the particulars.

We also know what it means to speak of a culture of lying. We can find ourselves in an environment where truth-telling is not much practiced, where people are expected to lie. One can imagine an organization whose new head punishes employees who fail to flatter her.

And we can imagine in a much larger sense that language could be co-opted to distort reality, highlighting some things, while hiding others from view. One thinks of such terms of art as *ethnic cleansing* for genocide or *collateral damage* for civilian deaths. In relation to abortion, whatever one's view on questions of legality, one can see why practitioners are trained to speak of the *products of conception*.

Considerations like these have led theologians to speak of *original sin*, a term first used by Augustine of Hippo.[6] We are not individuals first who subsequently enter into societies; rather, we rise up as individuals out of the midst of societies. We see this happening, at least in image, in a ceremony of baptism. Representatives of the community gather together. All social distance is collapsed, and out of the community comes the newly baptized person: the individual. And then that individual joins with the community to pray and, often, receive communion.

To paraphrase Alfred North Whitehead's notion of process: the community becomes one, and then it is one more.[7]

Since we come out of societies, we are not pure individuals who then, choosing to commit particular sins, stain our original purity and thereby diminish our humanity. No, we are touched by the wrongness of things before we are conscious of sin.

The social character of sin does not give us permission to stop caring about it. We should never become inured to the devastations brought about by murder, adultery, stealing, lying, disrespect, hatred of neighbor, anger, lust, desire of mere goods, and on and on. But seeing how we are caught in social webs and how even our own ways of thinking are entangled with deception, we realize: I can never fix this on my own.

I cannot even fix myself.

One must never stop desiring that evil come to an end! But the problem—it is as big as the universe.

Despite all our desires to the contrary, and despite its fundamental absurdity, we go on sinning.

He knows a friend is lonely. He knows he would enjoy talking to his friend. He has the time. But he sits, looking at his cellphone, flitting from screen to screen, from app to app, mindlessly. Why doesn't he make the call? He knows that tomorrow he will feel bad that he didn't call. What is keeping him back?

---

6. In Augustine, *Conf.* 5.9 (16); see translator Henry Chadwick's note in Augustine, *Confessions*, 82n13.

7. See Whitehead, *Process and Reality*.

One could do a psychotherapeutic investigation. Is it something from his childhood? Is he afraid of interrupting dinner or of being rejected—a fear that comes from somewhere else? Therapy might uncover deeper reasons why he is not reaching out to his friend. But even then, why is he allowing those deeper reasons to have control? He could get insights from therapy and still act in the same way or, rather, not act: still sit, scroll through his phone for an hour, and then off to bed, unhappy with himself, unhappy for his friend.

It makes no sense, and yet we go on doing it. Fortunately for us, God is more than our Creator. He is not happy to leave us alone in the mess of it.

In fact, quite apart from sin, he is not happy to leave us alone.

DISCUSSION QUESTIONS FOR CHAPTER 2

1. Has this chapter changed the way you would speak of sin? How so?
2. As you think about various sins—things done and left undone—does it seem helpful to think of them as holes in reality, as failures to be fully human? Why or why not?
3. What in the Bible do you find helpful in thinking about sin?
4. The author rejects the view that sin is a necessary step in our growing into mature humanity. What do you see as the strengths or weaknesses of that view?
5. The author concludes the chapter with a rather small sin—the failure to phone a friend. He claims that there is, in the end, no adequate explanation of that failure. Have you experienced sins where you could not understand why you did them, actions that, although you did them, you cannot explain why?

CHAPTER 3

God's Speech and God's Spirit

How God acts in the midst and the mess of things—God's desire to be with and alongside his creatures—God's Spirit as his promise from the future

Fasten your seatbelts; our adventure of faith is about to accelerate. We don't know why—indeed, it is impossible to know why—nevertheless, from the beginning, God has desired to be with his creatures. This is simply a given of biblical faith, a brute and inexplicable datum. God was not content only to create the world; he also wanted to be in the world, to be alongside the beings he had made.

To bring this about, he started talking.

It is a striking feature of the Bible, yet largely overlooked, perhaps from overfamiliarity, perhaps from failure to appreciate how weird God is. Yet if one came from a social context where the Bible was unknown or largely forgotten, a talking God would seem strongly counterintuitive and perhaps completely absurd.

Without the Bible, if one thinks God is the reason the universe started, and, having given it the first push, God stepped back and let the universe go—if one thinks God is like a watchmaker who winds up his finely crafted product and then allows it to tick away on its own—then one will not have a category for divine speech.

Watchmakers do not talk with watches. And even if they did, watches cannot talk back. Nor do chair makers talk with chairs. Symphony composers do not talk to their music—or if they do, they confirm they are themselves eccentric and weird. A great divide exists between maker and thing made, and even more so between Creator and thing created.

Much of our post-COVID world is also post-Christian. Long before COVID, many people were styling themselves as spiritual. Their beliefs are distant from the fundamental claim of biblical religion of divine speech. Indeed, right here, the Bible exposes a vast difference between being spiritual and being religious. People who like to say they are spiritual-but-not-religious mean to say they aren't tied down to the specifics of any given religion or religious text. And that means—sadly, it seems to me—they are deprived of the most remarkable claim in the Bible: the claim that God speaks.

Theologian Robert Jenson liked to point this out. In his late-in-life theological lectures, transcribed and then published as *A Theology in Outline*, this point is his first point. A person who wants to learn from the Bible about God has to start here: "The God of Israel is a talkative one. . . . The Jewish God cannot keep his mouth shut! He is talkative! And he moreover expects to be answered!"[1]

It's as if a chair maker wanted to be a chair alongside his other chairs and, at the same time, wanted to have a conversation with them. Don't tell me the God of the Bible isn't weird.[2]

In the Bible, God's talking—in the sense of him speaking to particular created beings—starts in the garden he created for the original human. Right after they have eaten from the tree of knowledge of good and bad, the text says: "And they heard the voice of the LORD God walking in the garden in the cool of the day" (Gen 3:8). Robert Sacks translates this as "strolling" and notes: "The word

---

1. Jenson, *Theology in Outline*, 15.

2. For more, see "The Weirdness of Divine Love," chapter 5, in Austin, *Friendship*. By "weird" I mean, as I say there, that God's desire to be with us and talk with us "is not only mysterious, unusual, or strange but also in a sense 'uncanny,' beyond our 'ken.'" But I do not mean to suggest "any sense of 'weird' that involves fate or the loss of freedom (as in the 'weird sisters' of Shakespeare's [*Macbeth*])" (49).

here translated as 'stroll' is a reflexive form of the root that means *to walk.* Strolling is like taking a walk; it is done for its own sake, rather than undertaken as a means of getting to a place. The verse goes out of its way to present God as merely happening along, not as having made his way there for the purpose of checking up."[3]

If he is not checking up, what is God doing? He is just walking. He has made the world and now he wants to be in it, alongside his creatures. He wants to be near and enjoy the company of Adam and Eve.

But such strolling is not good enough, and not only because of what Adam and Eve have just eaten. The text says, "They heard the voice of the LORD God." They *hear* God; they do not *see.* There remains a sort of distance between them and God, the distance that sight would overcome. We could speculate on what that distance is, but whatever it is, it will remain until God reveals his face to human beings—the subject, in effect, of the final two chapters of this book.

Nonetheless, the situation in the garden—that distance from God despite his nearness—is definitely complicated by the obvious guilt felt by Adam and Eve on account of their having eaten the forbidden fruit. They hide themselves when they hear God's words. What words did they hear? God's first recorded words spoken to particular human beings are these: "Where art thou?" (3:9).[4]

Significantly, the words they hear when God is strolling about are in the form of a question. God not only is with them as one who strolls about the garden; God speaks to them, and, as Jenson noted, this God expects an answer. A question implies a relationship, some kind of equality at least to the extent that one can reply, one can speak back. Again to repeat the obvious, chairs do not answer questions posed by their maker, nor do symphonies, nor do any products

---

3. Sacks, *Lion and Ass*, 36; italics in original.

4. In Gen 1, God speaks in each day of creation, and his speaking is what brings creation about. On the sixth day, he speaks to the human beings, telling them to have children and to rule over creation; he also tells them what they may eat. But none of this divine speech in Gen 1 is from God alongside his creatures, but rather from God as Creator. Similarly, in Gen 2:16–17, when God commands the original human concerning eating from any tree he wants except the tree of knowledge of good and bad, God is, indeed, commanding, that is to say, over the human and not alongside.

of human making.[5] By asking a question, God shows his desire to have some sort of common ground with these human beings.

Note the coincidence. The humans have messed up. God is there, strolling in the same garden with them, speaking to them, asking a question.

In the midst of the mess, the speech of God occurs.

Not only does God want to be in the midst of them, God also wants to be alongside them in the mess.

My point is double. It is, yes, because we have sinned and gone astray that God has come to save us and help us. He begins to save us and help us by speaking to us. That short question, "Where art thou?" is a brilliant tool for summoning God's interlocutors back to themselves and back to him. To answer him, they have to make an account of what they have done. They have to own up to it. They have to, as it were, face the music.

But my point is also that God is not there in the garden only to fix a problem. God is speaking to them in the mess that they have made because he was already there, already enjoying being with them.

The primordial conversation in the garden is but the beginning; much talk ensues. Over centuries and even millennia, this divine desire for reciprocal communication will persist, and the fellowship of God with the people to whom he talks will sometimes be close, sometimes not. Humans turn out to be complicated beings. God's purposes require a lot of talk, as one can see with merely a quick glance through the Old Testament. Here's an exceedingly partial list of those to whom he speaks after Adam and Eve: Noah; then Abram/Abraham, Hagar, Abimelech, Abraham's unnamed eldest servant, Isaac, Jacob, Laban; then Moses, Aaron, Balaam, the people of Israel as a whole (in the Exodus), Gideon, Samuel, Solomon; and

---

5. This is why it is dangerous to speak of making babies and better to speak of children in the traditional way as being begotten, not made; unlike chairs, children do speak back! For a still-timely discussion of the lurking dangers of manipulated human procreation, see O'Donovan, *Begotten or Made?*

then Elijah and many other prophets. There are also angels who speak to people—angels who, often, turn out to be God himself.[6]

When you trace the speech of God through the Bible, you are at the same time tracing the story of how God decided to fix the mess that sin had created. About a thousand years after Adam and Eve, human wickedness had multiplied to such an extent that it was everywhere. At that time, God determines to erase the world and start over. But before he can do that, his eyes fall on Noah, a righteous man. Seeing Noah, God realizes that to start over would be to destroy the good along with the evil. Hence he speaks to Noah, giving him instructions to build an ark.

In the event, Noah's righteousness turned out to be complex; he had a complicated heart, not to mention a mixed bag of sons. First thing after the flood, Noah offers sacrifice, a sacrifice for which God did not ask and which he finds at once pleasing and troubling; it makes him realize that "the imagination of man's heart is evil from his youth" (Gen 8:21). Henceforth, rather than trying to fix humanity as a whole, God chooses instead to put up with the mess and to work within humanity.

Ultimately, God chooses to build a special people with whom he would communicate. This people he calls to be distinct from humanity as a whole. To that end, they were to have a particular relationship with God, a communicative relationship that brought with it distinctive customs and morals and laws. God would educate his chosen people, form them, talk with them, and love them. At the end, when at length the time was ripe, they would be the blessing for the whole world.

God's "new way" was to be specially related to a part for the sake of the whole.[7]

---

6. For a brief instance, to Sarah: "Nay, but thou didst laugh" (Gen 18:15). For famous instance: the "angel of the LORD" stopping Abraham from sacrificing Isaac, saying "now I know . . . thou hast not withheld thy son, thine only son from me" (Gen 22:11–12).

7. I owe to Sacks the term *new way* for what God inaugurates with Abram. The term reminds those of us who are Christians that the new way in Jesus Christ was prepared by this earlier new way through Abraham.

By speaking in particular to Abram, God launches this new way of dealing with the problem of wickedness. He speaks to Abram at some length and over several decades. Abram, to whom God would give the new name Abraham, becomes the first founder of God's people, Israel. Israel later has a second founder, Moses, with whom God speaks also, beginning with the famous voice at the burning bush and continuing also in his case for many decades. The Bible has a special word for both Abraham and Moses. Each of them is called a friend of God. And what made them God's friends? God spoke to them and they spoke to God, face to face, as one speaks with a friend.

Friend, we see, is another word for what God desires. He wants speech with people who will be friends with him.

But in no way is divine speech exclusively with Abraham and Moses. Even a partial list, as we saw above, points to God's extensive, ongoing desire for the engagement of talk. A few hundred years after Moses, we find God speaking to the boy Samuel as Samuel sleeps in the house of the priest Eli. Over the subsequent centuries when Israel had kings, God often speaks to and through prophets. This speech is sometimes in words heard and sometimes in visions seen.

In these years, Israel develops a collection of poetry that is precious and central to its identity. These poems, the psalms, provide models of conversation between people and God. The psalms show us how much speech with God there can be and how much variety it can have. They remind us, in addition, that sometimes God goes silent. In certain cases (say, rebellion or apostasy) this silence might be understandable, but in others the cessation of God's communication is sheer mystery.

Psalm 44 is heartbreakingly direct about this. It begins with the happy remembrance of the great deeds God has done in the past. Then it turns to the present, which is a time of trouble: "You have rejected and humbled us . . . our enemies have plundered us." The speakers tell God he is making a bad deal: "You are selling your people for a trifle and are making no profit on the sale of them." And then the speaker is singular, as if all Israel has become one sorry individual: "My humiliation is daily before me." Nonetheless, they say, they have not forgotten God; rather, it is precisely because

33

of their faithfulness to God that they have been targeted for attack and plunder: "Indeed, for your sake we are killed all the day long; we are accounted as sheep for the slaughter." And then the punch line: "Awake, O Lord! why are you sleeping?"[8]

That it is right to read the Old Testament through the lens of divine speech is supported in the New Testament by the writer of the Epistle to the Hebrews. This letter opens with the remarkable reality of God's speaking, which is put as a trajectory aimed toward the incarnation: "God who at sundry times and in divers manners spake in time past unto the fathers by the prophets, hath in these last days spoken unto us by his Son" (Heb 1:1–2). The incarnation of the word of God climaxes the millennia-long drama of God doing that most ungodlike thing of speaking to his creatures.

What must be the case if God really can speak with us? On God's side, we have already noted it: God has a desire to be with us, to communicate with us, to reach across the Creator/creature divide. On our side, this requires that God transform us so that we are no longer mere creatures. God must give us grace, a word theologians use for any special gift from God that goes beyond simple creaturehood.

If you've been a Christian for a while, your normal conception of grace might be in terms of church things—things like sacraments, which indeed can be called "means of grace." Or you might think of grace in a sort of dichotomy with law, that by the law we are all doomed, since we are sinners, but God's grace is a gift of pardon and life. Both these ways of thinking about grace are valid, but they do not go deep enough. And in fact, the law/grace dichotomy is often used in a misleading way to undermine the truth that the law itself is a gift of grace.

Because: the fundamental reality of grace is God's reaching out to us across the Creator/creature divide. We know this must be going on whenever we find God speaking to us. Indeed, the law that is given to the people of Israel at Mount Sinai is, fundamentally,

8. Verses 9–10, 12, 15, 22, and 23. As noted earlier, all psalms are quoted from the (1979 US) Book of Common Prayer.

God speaking to them. It is grace itself, a joyous reality—as pious Jews celebrate when they dance ecstatically with the scrolls of the Torah.

None of us on our own, as mere creaturely human beings, could speak to God. As I have remarked above, Harry Potter cannot speak to J. K. Rowling, his author. Before we can hear God and before we can respond to God, God must lift us up and give us a certain equal standing with him. A theological word for this is *divinization*. It does not mean God turns us into gods—there can't be multiple gods, for the reasons given before—but it does mean God has accomplished something that is beyond our rational grasp, and yet, well, there we are: hearing God, speaking to God.

Has God spoken to you?

You may think not. The Bible, however, not only purports to tell about God speaking to people starting way back with Adam. It also purports to tell, to put down in print, words that God has said, as well as a lot of words that have been said back to him. The Bible as a whole—the record of this conversation that God has desired and sought after—is called, in an antique phrase, "God's word written." The point of the phrase is to distinguish the Bible from God's Word incarnate, Jesus Christ, while yet affirming that this record of a conversation is itself the speech of God, addressed to us, the readers—the listeners.

Which means: if you have listened to the Bible, you have listened to God speaking.

Any time you read the Bible, God is speaking to you.

And if you are in the midst of a mess, God is speaking to you in that mess.

In early March of 2020, shortly before everything shut down, a Starbucks barista surprised me by saying she had started reading the Bible. She knew I was a priest, but until that moment, we had never talked about religious things. She asked if there was anything in the Bible about what was going on with the virus; she had a sense that there was, but she didn't know where to look. I fumbled for a brief answer and was glad some months later to be able to sit down with her for a good talk about Genesis. But at the time, without quite putting it into words even to myself, I could see: her reading the Bible was God's reaching towards her.

Whatever the mess is, whatever the world is, God wants to speak to us from the midst of it, to speak to us side by side.

Towards the end of *The Waste Land*, T. S. Eliot has a few lines inspired by the experience of some early Antarctic explorers, that in the extreme conditions they encountered, they often sensed there was another person with them. In the poem, this becomes a question of who that third person is—there are only two people in the scene. Look at your companion, and that's all there is; look ahead, and you sense there is a third walking alongside.

When out for a morning run, I have sometimes had the illusion that there is another person just slightly behind me, running along with me. When I turn to look, of course, no one is there. It is doubtless just the sound of my own feet echoing and coming back to me. In similar fashion, one might interpret as illusion the sense the Antarctic explorers had of an additional person.

But what I do, instead, is this: I bring to mind that God is always wanting to be alongside me. Independently of any perfectly natural scientific explanation for that sense of being accompanied, there is this fundamental datum of faith.

He wants to be with us.

There is more to say. God also wants things to turn out well; he wants not only to be with us but for our mess to be overcome. God wants to be not only the author of the story, and a character in the story, but also to be the end of the story, to guarantee that the story will turn out to be a good one.

Let me put this in other words. Most of this chapter has tried to grasp the remarkable reaching across from Creator to creature, but that is only the half of it. There is a further dimension to God's desire to be with us, namely, that he has fulfillment in mind.

Which is to say, the mess of the world, brought about by human sin and in the midst of which God wants to be beside us, is not taken away merely by God's presence in it. God longs for a future consummation of the world in which every sin is really taken away. In this future, all reality must be transformed, so that evil can no longer impede us, so that our sins no longer hobble us. When all those holes in reality where there ought to be fully human beings have been filled in, when all evil has been removed, then all things can come to their fulfillment. This state of affairs is what the Bible ultimately calls "a new heaven and a new earth" in which God has made "all things new" (Rev 21:1, 5). *God's working towards that goal is what we mean when we speak of God the Holy Spirit.*

The word *spirit* is related to breath. In English, to perspire is literally to "breathe through." Sometimes an old-timer will say of Mrs. Jones, who died last week, that she expired—her breath departed from her. Jesus himself, in antique translations, expired when he "gave up the ghost" (John 19:30, ghost being an alternative English word for spirit).

The Holy Spirit is God's purposeful breathing through history. Jenson speaks of God's Spirit as "the breath of God by which he blows things around and so keeps Israel's history moving." In times of trouble, when the way forward is blocked, and so forth, "the same thing happens again and again. The *ruah* [spirit] of the Lord falls upon so and so, and thus takes over and rescues Israel."[9] The Spirit of God blows through the Bible, from Genesis to Revelation. God's Spirit is a wind blowing the story forward, keeping it moving towards its ultimate consummation.

God not only wants to talk with us, he wants to blow through us.

Thus Jenson can summarize each person of the Trinity in terms of an identity within a story. "Who is this God? Well, he is God the author of the story with his people. Who is this God? He is God settled into that story and an actor in it. Who is this God? He is the wind of God that moves history."[10]

9. Jenson, *Theology in Outline*, 50.

10. Jenson, *Theology in Outline*, 48.

I like to think of the Holy Spirit as the future of God. The Spirit situates God not only behind us, as the source of the world, and not only beside us, as one speaking to us, but also in front of us. God is already the future towards which we are moving.

The reader may note: this implies that time is, in some manner, in God. As Creator, God is, of course, not in time—temporality is a feature of created things. Nonetheless, it is not problematic (even though we cannot understand it) for us to say there is something like time within God.

For when we say God is timeless, we mean only that he is not in time as creatures are. Time has no control over God. But we do not mean God is indifferent or unfeeling or heartless or anything else that implies deathlike-ness. God is supremely alive, and his transcendence over time and over all created things in no way means he is inert or unmoving. Although God is transcendent, he is not static.

The future matters.

If I am reading a novel by an unknown author and the plot gets convoluted—I can't tell what's going on, characters seem not to be going anywhere—whether I keep going will depend on my faith in the author. Do I think the author knows what she is doing? Will she be able to breathe life into this languid, dull world she has started? I need to have faith that she is able to bring her fictional world to a satisfying end. Of course, faith in an author does not mean I expect to feel safe in her hands. She might well be leading to a tragic ending; her aim might be to reach deep in my heart and wrench something out of it. A good author is not a safe author! Nevertheless, I need to be able to trust that, in the end, we will have gotten somewhere.

A good story, Aristotle says, is one that develops surprisingly but fittingly. As we progress through the story, we will not have been able to anticipate every future turn in the road; but each turn, however unexpected, will be experienced as fitting. Retrospectively, at the end, we will see the journey of the plot as one journey, a whole thing that makes sense.

To have faith in the Holy Spirit is then to believe two things. First, that the story of my life, and the story of the creation as a whole, will in the end be indeed a story: not just one damned thing after another, not (as Macbeth, towards the end, reckons it is) "sound and fury, signifying nothing." This is another way of saying that God guarantees that life will be meaningful.

Second, the meaning of history will be good news for humanity. One could imagine an author having a brilliant vision such that, if we entrust ourselves to him, at the end of the story, we will have gotten somewhere; and yet, nonetheless, this author took us to a place we should not have gone. I sometimes feel, at the end of a masterful film, that my soul has suffered a certain harm through the experience. The very bloody end of the classic film *Taxi Driver*, for instance, is exceedingly satisfying: vengeance has been wrought on a whole network of evil characters, and good has won out. But to get to that point, one had to witness a lot of violence, and as Augustine says of soldiers coming back from war, the danger is that I will have enjoyed that infliction of violence.

There will be no such moral ambiguity at the end of the story towards which the Holy Spirit works. It will be satisfying and right, both cosmically and humanly.

There is much more that could be said about the Holy Spirit as the future of God, but we will limit ourselves here to one final point. Once the speech of God has become incarnate in Jesus Christ, the job of the Holy Spirit is to keep Jesus in our minds, to keep him before us. In a sense (here I again follow Jenson), Jesus has ascended into the future of God. The Holy Spirit makes that future present to us in an anticipatory way. Everything the Holy Spirit does—one might think, for example, of sacraments such as Holy Communion—is to present to us here and now a gift of the future.

The reader may well wonder if this book has, so far, begged the question of what is right and fitting for human beings. What does it mean for a story to be—as I wrote above—"satisfying and right . . . humanly"? This question is the provocation for our next chapter, wherein we turn to Jesus as the revelation of the human being.

DISCUSSION QUESTIONS FOR CHAPTER 3

1. Do you have a favorite psalm? (If not, pick up a Bible, read a few, and pick one.) What is the content of that psalm's speech? When you say that psalm, is there communication between you and God, and, if so, are you able to describe that conversation?

2. The author claims God is weird to want to speak with us. Do you think it is weird?

3. COVID-19 certainly added to the mess of life on earth. The biblical claim seems to be that God wanted to be with us in the midst of that mess. How did you experience, or how might you understand, God being with us in the time of COVID?

4. The author claims that God the Holy Spirit is linked to the future, that the Holy Spirit is God's assurance that his purposes will not ultimately be thwarted. (1) What does that mean in our own lives? (2) How might the Holy Spirit have been active in the time of COVID?

CHAPTER 4

Jesus' Life and Teaching

Behold the human!

Alexander Pope's line, a distinctively English iambic pentameter, is characteristically memorable and now proverbial: "To err is human; to forgive, divine."[1] Pope's poetic essay in which this line appears speaks not only to what makes a good literary writer but, more broadly, to what makes a good person. A key part of developing goodness is to be alert to the workings of pride. Pride obscures vision; we see clearly neither ourselves nor others; it causes us to make mistakes, to err.

Which is to say, we are sinners. We blind ourselves to what we ought to see, we do what we ought not to do, and we fail to do what we ought to do. For many reasons—pride, envy, lust, the whole jumble of vices—we fall short of what we ought to be. As we saw in chapter 2, our sin is a hole in reality; sin is an absence within ourselves.

But that is why Pope's line itself is errant. It misleads us into thinking that human beings are essentially sinners, that to be human is to be characterized by erring. This is a false conception. It

---

1. From Pope's long poem, published anonymously in 1711, *An Essay on Criticism*. The line appears late in pt. 2. Especially pleasing is the semicolon's pause at the suppressed middle stress in the line.

would make lousy poetry, yet, still, the truth is: "To err is to fail at being human."

On the other hand, there is truth in saying that to forgive is divine. It belongs to God to forgive sins, because only God can right the mess that our sinning has brought about. Nonetheless, it is also human to forgive, and sometimes downright inhuman to refuse. When we fail to forgive people, it's not because we aren't divine. Rather, we fail to forgive because we are, one and all, to some extent, human failures. We are, one and all, less than human.

What I mean to suggest here—and, at this point, it can only sound strange to the reader—is that, in the end, there can be no space between being fully human and living a divine life. To err is not to be human; to forgive is both human and divine.

If you want to see a real human being, you need to look at Jesus.

This truth derives from the basic Christian claim that Jesus is both God and human. He is a real man; there is nothing fake about him, nothing missing from him that belongs to being human. When we say Jesus is like us in all respects except for sin, we do not mean that he lacks something that we have; the truth is, rather, that he has what we lack! Our sinfulness, to repeat, is a hole in us where there ought to be something. There is no such hole in Jesus.

At the same time, Jesus is fully God. "And the Word was made flesh, and dwelt among us" is Saint John's statement of the climax of the movement at which we were looking in chapter 3. God's desire to be alongside his people, first heard in his speech early in Genesis, finally breaks through into actuality: God is alongside his people precisely in his Word who is the human being Jesus. God's speech was heard in the garden; in Jesus, God is seen, as well as heard. John affirms just this: "We beheld his glory, the glory as of the only begotten of the Father" (John 1:14).

Let me deal with a distraction that used to bother me, something that, I have found, worries a number of people. It seems to be a contradiction to say that Jesus is both God and man. Yet, if it is a contradiction, then aren't we Christians just believing nonsense?[2]

It is true that it would be a contradiction to say that Suzanne was both a fish and a woman. You cannot have the DNA of a human being and the DNA of a fish at the same time: you just have whatever DNA you have, and it is either that of a fish, or of a human, or perhaps of some sort of hybrid. Suzanne might be a woman; she might be a fish; she might be somehow half-woman and half-fish. What she cannot be is wholly a fish and wholly a woman.

But there is no DNA that characterizes God. Why? Because God is the Creator, not a creature. Things like DNA apply to creatures. Thus to say Jesus is fully God and fully a man is not to assert a contradiction.

You might think there are other, possible, lurking contradictions in this claim of the incarnation. For instance, Jesus in about AD 30 was a man who lived in a particular place. But God, we say, is everywhere. Again, it would be a contradiction to say that Pierre was in Paris and nowhere else—while, at the same time, Pierre was everywhere on earth. People are in only one place at a time.

However, this is not a contradiction when we speak of God. For God is everywhere, only in the sense that God creates everything and holds it in being (which actually just means creates). God is not everywhere as something extra in every space. In that room we have before imagined at Mar-a-Lago in Palm Beach, Florida, you might find an orange-haired former US president, Lady Gaga, Cher, and (should he still be alive) your grandfather. That's possible. But you won't find God alongside them sitting in his own chair and drinking seltzer water. God is not everywhere, in any physical sense. And that's why there is no contradiction with him being everywhere and Jesus, who is both man and God, being at a particular time in one particular place.

None of this takes away the oddness of the incarnation. But it can settle our minds to see that, by believing the incarnation, we are not committing ourselves to absurdity.

2. Tertullian (ca. 155–ca. 220), a cranky yet interesting early church writer, has been charged with saying "I believe because it is absurd." That was a misattribution, and it is a misunderstanding. The absurd cannot be believed.

So let's look at Jesus carefully. What Jesus does and what he teaches will show us what true humanity is. Jesus forgives, heals, rejects demons, links himself with others, tells stories . . . and gets killed. These are what a real human being does. If you are fully human, you will likewise forgive, heal, rebuke evil, connect yourself with other people, tell stories, and (in this world of sin) lose your life.

We will take these in sequence.

First: true humanity forgives.

A remarkable and early story in the Gospels of Matthew, Mark, and Luke showcases Jesus as a man who offers forgiveness. We will follow the version given in Matt 9:2–8. Some people bring a paralyzed man to Jesus. Jesus sees the faith of those people. He says to the paralyzed man, "Son, be of good cheer; thy sins be forgiven thee." Certain officials hear Jesus' words as blasphemy. Jesus, "knowing their thoughts," asks them whether it "is easier, to say, Thy sins be forgiven thee, or to say, Arise, and walk?" To show that he has authority to forgive sins, Jesus tells the man to get up and walk, which the man does. The people marvel and praise God for it.

This brief text raises many questions. There was, as scholar Robert Gundry flushes out, an underlying assumption of common Jewish thought of the time. "The Jewish view of illnesses as direct results of particular sins (cf. John 9:2) contributed to Jesus' pronouncing the paralytic's sins forgiven."[3] Gundry refers us to the opening of a lengthy episode in Saint John, where the disciples show that they hold this view themselves; they ask whose sin brought about a particular man's blindness. Jesus, in Saint John, shows he does not accept that view; he says the man's blindness was not the result of anyone's sin.

Still, there is some sort of connection of sin and sickness. In the story of the paralyzed man, Jesus says (a) there are sins, (b) the paralyzed man has them, and (c) he is forgiving them. The sign that they really are forgiven is that the no-longer-paralyzed man gets up

---

3. Gundry, *Matthew*, 163.

and walks. The release from sin and the release from sickness go together; indeed, when Jesus asks which is easier to say, I think he means the two sayings amount to the same thing.

So back to the beginning of this story in Saint Matthew. Why does it say that Jesus sees the faith of the people who bring the paralyzed man to him? What is the faith that he sees them having? It seems to be faith that he, Jesus, has God's power, that he can forgive and heal. But, doubtless, they would not have been able to put it into those words. Their action—bringing the man to Jesus—seems more a "faith in" than a "faith that": Gundry goes so far as to suggest Jesus sees their action as making an offering to him. They are offering the paralyzed man to Jesus for Jesus to act in the authoritative, powerful way that he can.

Insofar as Jesus here is manifesting his divinity, he does not seem to be an example to us of what we should do. But such a conclusion is wrong, as is given by the context of this section of Saint Matthew. Three chapters, 5–7, are the summary of Jesus' teaching that Matthew gives us as the Sermon on the Mount. The next two chapters, in which this story falls, are Jesus' actions. The paralyzed man whose sins are forgiven comes almost at the middle of Jesus' actions. And at the middle of Jesus' teaching was, correspondingly, the Lord's Prayer.

Jesus' teaching, at its center, is that we should ask God to "forgive us our debts, as we forgive our debtors" (Matt 6:12). After finishing the prayer, Jesus returns immediately to forgiveness: "For if ye forgive men their trespasses, your heavenly Father will also forgive you," and if not, not (6:14–15). We need not worry over the various nuances of debts, trespasses, and the general word sins: the point is that what human beings do for one another is also what God does for them.

The point is: to forgive is human as well as divine.

Where might we see human forgiveness in the story of the paralyzed man? It seems to me it resides in the premise of the story. There are people who bring him to Jesus. Who are these people? They are people who knew him. They and he would share in the common run of humanity, falling short, in various ways, of what we are supposed to be. At various times, they may have sinned against him and/or against each other, in a number of ways that

45

are common to us. And he, the paralyzed man, may have sinned against them. But when they bring him to Jesus, they are all acting as one. They are united in a desire that Jesus see this one person. To act in harmony with other people suggests, although it does not prove, that harmony exists with those other people; the picture of the group bringing the man could be a picture of the result of forgiveness being extended to each other.

And so it could be that when Jesus sees their faith, he sees that they have been praying "as we forgive our debtors." Maybe they heard his teaching. Maybe they took it to heart.

Forgiveness follows upon sin, and it reverses the damage sin has done. Fundamentally, sin is that hole in reality; forgiveness fills the hole. It is a process; it cannot happen instantaneously, for we human beings exist in time and space. Healing takes time. Later, Peter would ask, "Lord, how oft shall my brother sin against me, and I forgive him?" (Matt 18:21). It seems that even after we have been granted forgiveness, we are perfectly capable of turning around and sinning again against one another.

Forgiveness is also realistic: it does not deny the gravity of sin. Jesus' teaching includes the counsel to rebuke someone who sins against you. He does not tell us we should stay silent, make excuses, or deny that the sin was a sin. This teaching is not for our sake, but for the one who has harmed us. "Take heed to yourselves: if thy brother trespass against thee, rebuke him; and if he repent, forgive him" (Luke 17:3). An honest rebuke is inspired by the hope that it will lead to an honest repentance; the point of the first is to make possible the second. And again, the process may need a lot of time: "If he trespass against thee seven times in a day, and seven times in a day turn again to thee, saying, I repent, thou shalt forgive him" (17:4).

The end of forgiveness is to live with other people in such harmony that we are able to do ordinary, good human things, like carrying a sick person to a hospital.

The second thing we see in Jesus: true humanity heals.

Healing, as already noted, is connected with forgiveness, although the manner of its connection is complicated and not immediately obvious. The Gospels give us many more instances of Jesus healing than of Jesus forgiving; but it is important to remember that healing has a relationship to forgiveness.

This is because sickness, like sin, tends to separate us from society. A sick person is isolated. From sheer weakness, sick people are not able to do what they would do. They may need others to help them, or they may suffer alone, secluded from other people's sight. Lameness, for instance, can frustrate the desire to get to healing, as in the story that opens John 5. There was a pool whose waters would occasionally stir, and, at the time of stirring, the first person to get to the water would be healed. Near the pool "lay a great multitude of impotent folk [that is, sick, lacking power], of blind, halt, withered." Jesus there heals a man who had been waiting thirty-eight years but never had been able to get to the water in time.

It is not easy to interpret the premise of this story—as presented, it seems arbitrary—but it is easy indeed to map the story onto situations of limited health care in various parts of our world. Resources are finite. The very sickness one has (or the country one lives in, or the culture of one's neighborhood) might keep one from being able to get to the resources before they run out. Unlike the paralytic of Matthew 9, the man whom Jesus heals in John 5 had no companions to bring him to healing when that was available. Saint John records an interesting detail. Jesus, on his own initiative, goes over to talk with the man. In a situation where a person was isolated and "impotent," he still was not isolated from Jesus.

The point of healing is to overcome isolation, so that the healed person may join in common human activities. Aristotle famously says that an isolated human being is not really human. Someone "who is unable to live in society, or who has no need because he is sufficient for himself, must be either a beast or a god."[4] That insight about human nature—that we belong in situations where we work

---

4. Aristotle, *Pol.* 1.2 (1253a28).

and play and live alongside one another—permeates Christian theology, and it underlies all the healings that Jesus does.

Returning to the events of Matt 8, one can recognize three facets of this healing-as-restoration-to-society in Jesus' first three healings. 1) A leper is cleansed of his isolating and contagious skin disease; Jesus sends him to the priest, according to the law, for restoration to his religious community (8:2–4). 2) Jesus heals the servant of a centurion, which he does at a distance, upon the request of the centurion himself. This is a healing that crosses boundaries: the centurion is not a Jew, although his approach to Jesus seems to indicate that he is at least friendly to Jewish faith. Jesus recognizes in him great faith, epitomized in his declaration that to have authority is to be under authority (something the centurion sees that both he and Jesus have). The healed servant will now be able to work under, and with, the centurion again; he is restored to function in a humane order that is outside Israel proper (8:5–13). 3) Jesus goes to the home of Peter and heals Peter's mother-in-law of a fever that had confined her to bed, and which, of course, could easily have turned deadly. He "touched her hand, and the fever left her: and she arose, and ministered unto them" (8:14–15).

Healing is always restoration to society, to communion with other people, whether in the home of a follower of Jesus, or the home of a foreigner, or in a city.

Disease as isolation is felt by individuals and those who may be near them, but, in a pandemic, it is felt, excruciatingly, by all. The decision of almost every government in the world to impose restrictions on human movement reminded us that one basic purpose of government is to provide for the public safety. This is true even though, as I became increasingly persuaded, many officials confused providing for public safety with extreme caution. David Leonhardt of the *New York Times* wrote in May 2021, concerning the Center for Disease Control's continued cautions against being outdoors without a mask: "There does not appear to be much scientific reason that campers and counselors, or most other people, should wear a mask outdoors all summer. Telling them to do so is an example of extreme caution—like staying out of the ocean to avoid sharks—that seems to have a greater cost than benefit." He went on: "Everything has downsides. And it is the job of scientific experts and public-health officials to help the rest of us think clearly about the benefits and costs of our choices."[5]

People will continue to disagree about the measures imposed at various times and places during the COVID period; they are worth impartial study, especially in preparation for a future world health crisis. The challenging thing about COVID was the difficulty of untangling appropriate care for public health from excessive fear of taking on risks. Isolation itself is harmful to human beings; lockdown will always be harmful, and its various harms need to be taken seriously, even as we also recognize the lethality and other serious harms (less than lethal yet still serious) posed by an ongoing pandemic.

Post-COVID, Christians can see something newly important in Jesus' healings that was always there: the point of healing is to restore human fellowship. It is not to bring us into a risk-free world but, rather, into a world where we live together and, together, carry out the things that are appropriate for us to do.

Third: true humanity rejects demons.

After the leper, after the centurion's servant, after Peter's mother-in-law, it is those with demons who are brought to Jesus. "When the even was come, they brought unto him many that were possessed with devils: and he cast out the spirits with his word" (Matt 8:16). What are we to make of being "possessed with devils"? What are demons?

Whatever they are, Jesus casts them out of the people they possess, and he is able to cast them out simply with his word. His actions make clear there is a distinction between people and whatever devil or devils that might possess them. The demonic is not the human; a person who has a devil acts in ways for which she is not responsible, that is to say, her actions are not truly her actions but something else that is working inside her.

5. David Leonhardt, "The Morning," email from the *New York Times*, sent out May 26, 2021.

Second, the possession that a devil may have over a person turns out to be temporary. The word of Jesus is able to drive out the interloping devils. In Matt 8:16, many who are possessed with devils are brought to Jesus, and he casts out every devil, without exception.[6] The exorcisms that Jesus performs liberate the humans, so that they can act freely with other people, as human beings do when they flourish. It is interesting to ponder why they had to be brought to Jesus and how that bringing to Jesus was done. Perhaps their friends had to constrain them from violent action; or perhaps they wanted to come to Jesus yet, at the same time, resisted coming to him, not being of a single mind; or perhaps the possession paralyzed them. The Scriptures indicate there were many different ways possession could affect a person, but, whatever it was in these particular persons, the persons had to be brought to Jesus. Having friends who care for you is, here, a necessary condition for liberating healing to occur.

In general, the Bible depicts the world as including inhabitants that are spiritual beings. There are hints that a spiritual creation preceded the physical one; that the members of that spiritual creation are what we mean when we refer to spirits or angels; that those members have freedom, and each of them has made a decision whether to be with or against God. The spiritual beings who rebelled acquired the name of devils or demons; they were defeated by Michael the archangel and cast out of heaven; they are mysteriously wrapped up with human sin; and, at the end, they will be locked up forever.

As a theological matter, one can interpret the biblical data in a nonliteral way. Such an interpretation would have demonic possession in the Scriptures refer to phenomena that we understand as mental illness or neurological disease of one sort or another. On this interpretation, when Jesus healed those possessed with demons, he was healing mental illnesses; driving out demons was thus a special case of Jesus' general healing ministry.

One might go further and, for instance, interpret angels not as spiritual beings in themselves but as particular instances of God

6. Gundry notes that this is a particular emphasis of Matthew's shaping of this verse (Gundry, *Matthew*, 149).

speaking to people. Famously, Gen 18 is a story of three visitors who come to Abraham; they are men; they seem to be angels; and, as the narrative continues, they seem to be one character, namely, God himself. Later (in the famous episode we noted in the last chapter) when Abraham is about to sacrifice his son, an angel stops him, but the words that the angel speaks at that time refer to himself, the speaker, as God: "And the angel of the LORD called unto him . . . and said . . . thou hast not withheld thy son, thine only son from me" (Gen 22:11–12). So there is scriptural ground available if one wants to interpret the so-called spiritual creation as a way of dealing with God's communicative desire, without going so far as to affirm the reality of the spiritual creation per se.

And so I used to think. In those days, I would point out also that, in the creeds, we make no affirmations of faith concerning angels or devils, either one. But now I think I was trying to explain away too much, and that it is better to hold that angels and demons in fact do inhabit our world, and that the Scriptures show us truth about them. That is to say, it seems to me an easier and overall more coherent position to hold that there is a spiritual creation. Nonetheless, dear reader, if you disagree, your view is within the bounds of Christian orthodoxy, as, for instance, laid down by the creeds.

Now, if we hold that demons are actual spiritual beings, how are we to understand being possessed by them? Something is really there, something that is described in frightening terms (see, e.g., Matt 8:28–34). But this does not mean that there is ever possession such that a human being loses the ability to turn to Jesus (remember the friends). Nor is there any demon who can do other than obey when Jesus speaks to him.

True humanity is not afraid of demons. Because of our finitude (lack of knowledge, lack of experience) and because of our sin (our lack of full humanity), we may not be able to drive away that which is demonic. But neither need we run away from it. At the end, when the man had been liberated and restored to his right self, the crowds were afraid and asked Jesus to go away (Matt 8:34). True humanity is not to be afraid like that. We can find ourselves alongside Jesus, who himself sits alongside the one who had been possessed but is so no longer.

❖ ❖ ❖

And so to the fourth point: true humanity links itself with others. Jesus deliberately sees, touches, speaks to, and eats with people whom others did not see or touch or address or commune with: children, women, foreigners, and sinners (of whatever sort).

Our first three points have been leading up to this one. To forgive, to heal, to drive out evil spirits: all of these are actions aimed at restoring afflicted people to a place of connection in the world.

Jesus links himself, ultimately, to every human being. It is not a new sentiment; the Roman playwright Terence, in the second century BC, wrote, "I am human, and therefore I reckon nothing human to be alien to me."[7] That Terence's line has become proverbial—among many others, Maya Angelou is noted for quoting it—shows that people aspire to have universal human connections, connections that overcome long-standing differences and hostilities. But the Gospels show something more in Jesus: they show the actual overcoming of difference.

Just as, in Jesus, God has reached across the Creator/creature distinction and spoken to us as a person human beings actually saw, so Jesus reaches across all human divisions to touch humanity wherever a human being is to be found. In this light, there is no sentimentality when Jesus says "Suffer little children to come unto me" (Luke 18:16) or when he calls a child to him and sets him as an example of humility for his disciples (Matt 18:2–4). Jesus puts children on a par with himself, as one who embraces humility for the sake of serving others; children are not excluded from his reach.

Neither are women, neither are tax collectors, neither are sinners, neither are Samaritans or other foreigners. There is no need to elaborate the point further: restored humanity is a humanity that desires, and works for, connections with all humanity, and such connections are made via Jesus, the one, true, fully human being.

❖ ❖ ❖

7. Author's translation of "*Homo sum, humani nihil a me alienum puto*," in Terence, *Heauton Timorumenos*.

The fifth point is that true humanity tells stories. I say this, first off, because Jesus' characteristic mode of teaching was by telling stories. But there is a deeper point here.

It was not necessary for God to send his Son in order to save us from our sins. God could have saved us in a lot of different ways. He could, for instance, have sent us a letter. But, as Aquinas says, it is particularly fitting that he sent his Son. Why is it more fitting for Jesus to come to us as a human being than for God to drop a message in our inbox?

Recall the early days of COVID. We did not know much about the disease, but we knew it could be deadly. As a result, extreme precautions were taken to limit contact. A friend of mine told me of an elderly and faithful couple in her congregation who fell sick, were quarantined in their home, and then, in short order, were taken to a hospital. At least they got to share a room, so they did not suffer their sickness alone. They were denied all visitors: no family, no clergy, no friends. Their daughter, who lived out of state, besought the priest to try to visit them. But there was no way. All that could be done was a connection, a one-time connection, via iPad. A nurse, fully covered in protective clothing, held an iPad in front of the face of the husband and then the wife. They could see the priest, although by this time they were not able to speak. They could hear the priest's voice. The entire conversation, which had been hard to arrange at all, had to be done within ten minutes. The man died a day or so later. His wife held on for a few days after that. Their funeral was long delayed, in part on account of rather severe restrictions. The priest shared not only this story with me but her sense of how awful the whole situation was.

The difference between God sending a message and God coming to us in the flesh is the difference between an iPad visit and visiting in person. Although we understand the restrictions we had to live under—it is no part of my argument that any particular restriction was unwarranted—we know in our soul the difference between a message and an in-person visit. Jesus does not say to the sheep on his right hand, "I was sick, and you stayed at a safe distance." That is to say, we feel (or, at least, I would say we should feel) that there is something wrong about not being able to make personal visits. Even if the restrictions are right and necessary in the circumstances, we should not lose our sense that something is wrong.

I have just passed on a story about a couple, a priest, and the ministrations of the church. To be human means to share stories. It is by means of stories that we come to understand things, and perhaps thereby we can be changed. Jesus could have given simple information: God loves you. Pay attention to children. Don't let old feuds control your behavior. Why did he tell stories?

Because he wanted to bring us within God's being, to lift us up to God's level. Jesus was interested in changing us. The biblical diagnosis of the human predicament is that we have hard hearts. Where there ought to be flesh, there is stone. This was understood by the great prophets of Israel[8] and grieved Jesus when he encountered it.[9] One of the ways stony hearts are turned into living hearts is by means of stories.

There is a great one in 2 Sam 12:1–7. The prophet Nathan tells David the king about a poor man who had just "one little ewe lamb" who "was unto him as a daughter." A rich man, rather than killing one of his own flock, took that poor man's lamb to provide a meal for a guest. Nathan doesn't conclude the story, doesn't ask a question, doesn't state a moral; he simply tells that bit of a story. David is angered and cuts into his telling: "The man that hath done this thing shall surely die." Whereupon Nathan says, "Thou art the man."

As Hamlet himself would try, but without the purpose of changing a heart: "The play's the thing / Wherein I'll catch the conscience of the king."[10] Nathan does catch the conscience of the king, and David acknowledges his wrong—both adultery and murder—and repents; he takes his medicine. It is bitter, and it marks the rest of his life, but we admire his character in his repentance; perhaps even more, we should admire Nathan and the power of a story.

---

8. See, for instance, Jer 31:33–34, where God promises to write his law on the heart, with the result that it will no longer be necessary to teach the law; this is fulfilled when Jesus gives the Holy Spirit, who indeed writes God's law on the heart. See also Ezek 36:26, where God's promise is explicitly to replace the stony heart with a heart of flesh; the new heart is here, rather clearly, God's Spirit.

9. See, for one of many instances, Mark 3:5.

10. The final lines of act 2.

It, of course, needs to be a true story. False stories—false by omission, by slant, or by deceit—can harm us. The cry of "fake news" is actually a cry of "false stories," and, in turn, the cry of fake news can itself be a false story. We are clearly in need of good human stories today, stories that shine with the truth about humanity.

That's why the stories of Jesus are of great human importance. To be fully human, we need to be telling the stories of Jesus and, also, to see stories today that are illuminated by his story. If you, good reader, are an artist, a public speaker, a writer, or in some other way a crafter of narrative, the world needs you to apply your gifts right here. And all of us need to notice and tell everyday stories that shine with light reflected from the Gospels.

Finally: true humanity gets killed.

I have quoted Herbert McCabe a couple of times already; let me do so again. McCabe liked to say that Jesus shows us a human being who lives entirely by love (that was McCabe's way of saying Jesus is fully human). Therefore, *of course*, he gets killed. In a fallen world, a true, a full human being is a threat to the entire structure of things that is built upon fear, hatred, distrust, and putting self-protection above all else. There was no inevitability that Judas would do the deed, or the Jewish authorities, or the imperial agents of Rome; it could have happened in some other way. But that fallen humanity would seek to exterminate a man who lived by love, that was (and remains) inevitable.

Jesus puts it memorably when he says if you love your life, you will lose it. Interestingly, in the Greek, the word is not *love* but *save*, which is, of course, related to safety: "For whosoever will save his life shall lose it" (Mark 8:35/Luke 9:24). To save your life is to seek to preserve it; it is to seek safety for yourself. There is no surer way of losing your soul—the word here translated *life* is *psyche* (soul)—than to put safety first.

To learn to be human is to learn to live in a way that is not afraid of death. This means, most of all, not to be afraid of living as a testimony to Christ, even if there are economic or social costs to doing so. Christians are not supposed to seek martyrdom, but should we be living in a place and a time where Christians are still martyred, we should not strive to avoid that outcome at all costs.

Death will come to us all, but, nonetheless, we do not seem to know how to talk about it or prepare for it. Some people want to take charge of their own deaths, to control the means and the timing; this desire, celebrated as a healthy realism, pushes back against a widespread denial of death, manifest not only in reluctance to speak about dying but in extensive, often uncomfortable medical treatments that are no more than grasping after straws. But these two alternatives are both inhuman; both fail to achieve what a fully human being should be. We humans are mortal, but our mortality is not something over which we have the final say.

It comes as fresh air to read older spiritual books on holy dying, to read old prayers of people asking God to help them be prepared for their death when it comes. And there are a few novels of a more contemporary sort that also embrace this wisdom; for instance, *The Good Husband*, by Gail Godwin, whose main character, learning of her likely terminal breast cancer, decides to forgo treatment in order to spend the final bit of her life preparing for its end. But I have a real-life example.

It is my father. A believer all his life, he had had some bouts with cancer that he won, persisting through the treatments with courage and faith. Then, when he was in his mid-eighties, cancer reappeared, spreading rather quickly, ultimately in his lungs. With his doctor's advice, he did not try to defeat the cancer this time; the treatments would have been of uncertain benefit but of quite certain bodily harm. He told everyone who asked that the good Lord had given him a long life with many blessings of wife, family, friends, and that he was ready now to go see Jesus. He checked himself into an "old folks' home" (as he called it); my mother drove there and was with him every day (bringing his clothes home to launder them herself). And about a month later, at the age of eighty-eight, he died.

He inspires me to be faithful and to persist but also to acknowledge that a time will come for me to turn myself over to other hands.

Dying can come suddenly; one of the old prayers asks God to save us from sudden death, that is to say, dying without being prepared. There is nothing inhuman about putting one's affairs in order. A few years ago, I was at a retreat sponsored by the pension fund of my church; one speaker advised us to make a folder labeled "When I Die" that contains information (say, bank account numbers) for my children. This isn't morbid; it's human. It's like having your suitcase packed for a journey you know you'll be taking, although you don't know when.

Dying reveals an important characteristic of full humanity. Full humanity is vulnerable. It does not try to be in control of everything right to the end. It greets the morning with praise: "This is the day which the LORD hath made; we will rejoice and be glad in it."[11]

But on the way to death, there can be much loss. We should not be embarrassed by diminished faculties. There is nothing undignified about caring for someone who needs wiping and washing and feeding and so on, nothing inhuman about receiving such care from another.

There is also no loss of dignity when one is rejected by others, accused falsely of doing terrible things, misunderstood, reviled, even tortured. Nothing anyone can do to us will take away our humanity. Betrayed by Judas, abandoned by frightened disciples, berated by interrogators through the night, brought from a religious trial to an imperial one, subjected to whipping, to thorns pushed into his flesh, bloodied, perhaps with swollen eyes, twisted face, lost teeth—the governor put a cloth over him and made him stand wearing his thorn-crown in the sight of all the people. And what was it that Pilate the governor said? They were words both ironic and deep, words that have stuck with us for two thousand years and more.

"Behold the man!"[12]

Even in that extremity, even just hours before his death, Jesus shows us what it is to be a man, to be fully human.

11. Ps 118:24, here quoted in the translation of the 1662 Book of Common Prayer.

12. John 19:5. Paintings that assist meditation on this revelation of true humanity can be found easily by googling "Ecce homo." They range from sentimental to grotesque, from pained to placid, and show how these words of Pilate capture, however unintentionally, the whole human world.

DISCUSSION QUESTIONS FOR CHAPTER 4

1. The author claims that Jesus shows us what full humanity is. He identifies six characteristic actions of full humanity: to forgive, to heal, to rebuke evil, to connect yourself with other people, to tell stories, and to die. Which of these seems most important to you? Conversely, which seems least important? Is anything missing in this list?

2. Suppose, a few centuries in the future, scientists find a way to keep people from ever dying. Would that be a good thing? Why or why not?

3. When Jesus on the cross prays "Father, forgive them; for they know not what they do" (Luke 23:34), he connects the beginning and the end of this chapter, namely, forgiveness and dying. Is this a significant connection or just a happenstance? Is it easier to forgive people if we remember we are going to die? Or (the other way around) is it easier to die if we have forgiven people?

CHAPTER 5

Jesus' Death and Resurrection

Behold our true friend!

"He was dead as a doornail on Friday and alive on Sunday." "He was dead, really dead. Then he rose out of the grave to life. And I have bet my life upon it."

A young adult remembers certain lines for the rest of his days. I was in college, new to the Episcopal Church, looking up to the pulpit where our rector was speaking. "Doornail." "Friday . . . Sunday." He was the Rev. Donald L. Campbell, the first Episcopal priest I listened to, and I reckon I heard well north of a hundred sermons from him during my college years in Santa Fe. Of all those sermons, I remember just a few lines, this one above all. The death was as real as a doornail—indeed, among his death's instruments were large and awful nails. And then: Sunday, life.

Half a dozen years later, a student at seminary, with my little family squeezed into a tight pew of the hugely majestic Saint Thomas Church in New York City, another priest high in a pulpit, this one I did not know—we were just visiting—proclaimed the reality of Jesus' death and resurrection, and added his forceful personal declaration: "I have bet my life upon it." He was the Rev. John Andrew, who was able (I later learned), in terms often personal, to insinuate that human life is high drama. My wife and I both thought that here he was right, that although we had not thought of it this way, we, too, had bet our lives on it.

Both these priests, as well as my wife, are now dead, dead as doornails, I suppose I could say, at least in terms of their mortal bodies. The Christian hope is for resurrection from the dead, but, aside from Jesus, that resurrection yet lies in the future. Still, we believe that the dead are alive in some mysterious way, that what they bet their lives upon has proven true—that God himself has proven true. Truth is more than a characteristic of a statement; it is, or can be, a characteristic of a person, as when we say of someone: "She is a true friend."

To die as a Christian is to believe that the most important events of all human history took place at a cross and a nearby tomb over three days some two thousand years ago—and that, in these events, God has proven true.

We are speaking of the events of the death and resurrection of Jesus. What are these events?

First, his resurrection. It was not a resuscitation. Resuscitation does sometimes happen, at the hands of lifeguards, say, or in some near-death experiences. There are also resuscitation events in the Scriptures, performed, for instance, by the Hebrew prophets Elijah and Elisha, or, for later instance, in the book of Acts. Jesus himself resuscitated people who had died. Saint John tells of a man named Lazarus, who was dead and buried and had been such long enough for his body to smell. Indeed, Martha warns Jesus of that very fact: "By this time he stinketh."[1] Jesus, undeterred by things that stink, summons Lazarus back to life. Naturally, there was great rejoicing. But Lazarus was returned to the same sort of life as he had before he died, the same sort of body, a life of contingency and a body vulnerable to disease and aging. Lazarus would die again.[2] He did not have a resurrection, but only, as it were, a reprieve.

1. John 11:39, here being a delightful example of the pungency one can find in the antique language of the King James Version.

2. The only case I know of speculation to the contrary is from Walter Miller who, in his *Canticle for Leibowitz*, makes Lazarus a character who has never

Although what happened to Jesus is different from all these cases, the body with which he rose from the grave has material continuity with the body that was nailed to the cross, the body that was initially conceived in Mary's womb, the body that had gone through all the stages of normal human development into manhood. The resurrection body is *that* body; it is the sort of thing that can be pointed to. That's why many of the resurrection accounts emphasize that the tomb was empty—at least, empty of him. What was found in the tomb is variously reported: gravecloths, two angels, a young man, two men, an angel sitting on the stone. The singular constant in all the reports is that the body is not there; Jesus is not there.[3]

Hence we say (generalizing from Jesus to all humanity), the resurrection body has material continuity with the earthly body. It is not a brand-new body with no connection to the old; if it were, it would mean that, if only you knew the right place to look, you could find the old one, discarded. The earthly body is not like the skin of a snake, something to be shed, to slide out of. Paul writes that he longs not to be rid of this body but to be further clothed. We groan, he says, not "that we would be unclothed" (i.e., get rid of our earthly body) "but clothed upon." Paul's insight points to this claim of material continuity: "that mortality might be swallowed up of life" (2 Cor 5:4).

The body of the resurrection is not a new suit of clothes; rather, it is made out of the old suit of clothes. It is made from the old body. But what a making! In resurrection, the body is changed—mysteriously, awesomely, beyond all earthly experience. The characteristics of the new body are captured obliquely in the various resurrection stories. The resurrected Jesus eats, he touches, he breathes, he converses with his disciples, he walks, and he does many other ordinary human things. And yet: he appears in rooms without coming through doors. He seems to be able to get from one place to another just about instantaneously, as if he did not have to traverse the distance between. He is different, while still being the

---

died; indeed, he was that mysterious wanderer mentioned above in ch. 1. Although vulnerable to pain and injury, Lazarus is still alive more than a thousand years in *our* future. It is a state of affairs that does not make him happy.

3. See Matt 28, Mark 16, Luke 24, and John 20.

same as he always was. Material continuity underlies the magnificent transformation.

God's Holy Spirit is key to this transformation.

The risen Jesus is a person who, thanks to the Spirit, has come from the future to be in the present. What I mean is this: he has the sort of body that will characterize all God's children in the resurrection life that, for all the rest of us, both the living and the dead, still lies in the future. It is a body not subject to contingency, not vulnerable to accident, disease, and aging, a body whose aliveness will come not by its own powers but by God's Spirit. N. T. Wright likes to point out that this is Paul's meaning in 1 Corinthians 15:42–44 when Paul speaks of a spiritual body. The translation misleads, Wright says; we should think of a body that is made alive by the Spirit. The resurrected body is the Spirit-powered body.[4]

All this is meant by Jesus' resurrection—this and much more, more than any of us could put into words, even if we had unlimited time and unbounded literary skill. He who was dead on the cross has risen from his grave and is now alive in such a way that he will never die again.

You can bet your life on it.

What, then, about his death?

Let us contrast it with his resurrection. What happened on Easter morning was a unique event, never before known to human history and still to this day unrepeated. What happened on Good Friday, by contrast, is what happens all the time.

We know death. We know the slow death of an elderly person whose inhalations are labored, and then spaced further apart, and then cease. We know the death of a child in a pediatric ICU, afflicted with a difficult condition that proved, in her case, incurable; holding her hand, we have seen the crests of the EKG monitor get further apart, and weaker, and gradually turn flat. We know the sudden death of a bullet. We know death from a car crash. And, in recent times, we know death from COVID.

4. Wright, *Surprised by Hope*, 155–56.

In the last chapter, I said that Jesus teaches us that to be human is to die. The way we experience death is shaped by the sin of the world: bullets, environmentally caused cancers, and engineered viruses (whether SARS-CoV-2 was one or not, does not matter here)—these things shape the pain and sadness with which death surrounds us.

It is a long-debated question among theologians whether Adam and Eve would have died, had they not sinned. Is death in the world solely because of human sin (and the deep, complex relationship of sin and illness, as Jesus' healings claim)? Or would there have been death anyway?

Who knows? In any event, it is impossible for us to imagine human life without death. For what would it mean not to die? Would one have children? Would one grow, would one age? Would there be stages of life? The whole question is so hypothetical, so far-fetched, that it is nigh impossible to say anything true or illuminating. The world we have is the only world we know. In this world, the evidence is mixed. Some of the dying that happens, it appears, is not connected with sin but seems to be just the consequence of us having finite bodies that age and wear out in various ways. And other death seems more closely connected with sin.

Jesus' own death, the one that really happened to him, was clearly precipitated by sin. I believe it was precisely his sinlessness, his perfect humanity, that marked him for destruction. Bad people are always enemies of the good, because the good is an implicit rebuke to their self-satisfaction. Dear reader, never become complacent with your sins! Defend yourself from wrongful attack, yes, but when the truth is spoken—when you are convicted in your own heart—do not suppress that! Some people have thought that Pilate was wavering about Jesus, that he came close to a conversion of heart. He could tell that Jesus understood him, understood his heart. He saw that Jesus, implicitly, offered him another way of life. Pilate wavers, but then he suppresses the disruptive thoughts. "What is truth?" he asks (John 18:38)—a question that, it seems to me, marks his return to self-protective cynicism.

The death that Jesus actually died is because of sin. And yet he takes to the cross with himself not only other victims of rigged

63

judicial processes, and victims of bullets and hatred and deceit, everyone who dies because of the sins of others—but, also, he takes to the cross every human being in his or her death. While it is true Jesus died because of sin, it is also true that he died because we die.

The death of Jesus is the most tragic event of human history. And yet it is also the most ordinary event in human history. Tragic, because he was supremely innocent and undeserving. Ordinary, because it happens to every one of us.

We closed the last chapter with Pilate's words when he brings Jesus out before the jeering crowd: "Behold the man!" But the interpretation Jesus gives of his own death is different. To follow Jesus' interpretation is to see deeper into what humanity is. It is to look at the cross and say: Behold our true friend!

The word *true* is there because it is not merely a true statement to say that Jesus died. He died in the best way, being true to the end. But, at the end, there is something newly actualized, and that something is captured by the word *friend*.

Jesus interpreted his death the night before, when at supper he said, "Greater love hath no man than this, that a man lay down his life for his friends" (John 15:13). Those words were a gift to his disciples, so that they would know, when it happened, what his death meant—namely, that it was an act of love, the greatest act of love, given for his friends.

This seems to have stunned the disciples. Readers of the Bible never know, when a speech goes on, whether there was a pause in it, whether the speaker hesitated in some expectation of a response. If Jesus paused after John 15:13, the disciples were literally speechless. But if they were stunned, what were they stunned by? Intuiting that Jesus' death was immanent? Or that he says he is dying for his friends?

As Jesus continues, it's as if he has grasped their amazement, and that would explain his making explicit what he had just implied. He connects the dots. He says, "Ye are my friends" (15:14), as if in answer to an unstated question.

This word *friend*, rare but significant, has been saved for this moment. Although friendship is an underlying current from the start, Jesus has never before called them his friends. The reader can infer the silent drama of the heart: they sense he is going to die; he states that the greatest love is to die for one's friends; they wonder if by friends, he means them; and, finally, he states it plainly: Ye are my friends. He is going to lay down his life for them, and that means they really are his friends.

We all sense, I think, that to have a friend is the most significant relationship a person can have (even though we are often confused about what friendship really is). When that friendship comes from Jesus, however, it is a stupendous offer of intimacy. Jesus explains: He will no longer call them his servants (or slaves; the Greek can be translated either way). Why not? Because servants do not understand what their master does, they merely do as told; "but I have called you friends" (15:15).

Jesus offers the intimacy of sharing with them everything he thinks, everything he knows, his whole perspective on reality. He completely opens himself to them; he offers for them to share with him a common mind. Jesus has explained to them what he is doing, so that now they can understand things as he does—which means they are his friends. It's as if they are inside his mind.

Or better, that he has put his mind inside them: "For all things that I have heard of [from] my Father I have made known unto you" (15:15).

Step back a bit for the big picture. As God's Son, Jesus receives everything he is from his Father. His obedience is real obedience, not blind, because he and the Father share a common mind. They are at one about things. It is this mind, the mind Jesus has from the Father, that he now has shared with his disciples.

The end of this post-COVID catechesis is the end of all Christian teaching, because it is the end of all God's work. I conclude with a few briefly stated observations.

In our present time of rebuilding, Christian teaching needs to celebrate friendship, to aim at friendship, and to encourage one another in the practices of friendship. Our true friend on the cross shows us two things about human friendship that need to be planted in our hearts. First, real friends become such through the intimacy of sharing their minds (their hearts, their souls) with one another. Second, real friends are willing to die for one another.

The death of Jesus is his making himself our friend. The resurrection of Jesus is his making our friendship with him something that is stronger than death.

Friendship is a great key for reinterpreting the entire Bible. Human beings were created to live with one another as friends. The fall results in the loss of universal friendship. God works to restore friendship in exemplary ways in the people of Israel. In Jesus, God's intentions are brought to their fulfillment. And the consummation of all things will be the holy city, come down from heaven to earth, wherein people are fully human, living without sin—which is to say, living as friends.

To be fully human in the world that God has actually created is to live in friendship with others. None of us can do that perfectly, since friendship takes time (and time, in this world, is finite), and since sin, as we now see, is the very opposite of friendship. But one point is clear: when the kingdom comes in its fullness, all the friends of Jesus will be friends with all the friends of Jesus.

The defining characteristic of that kingdom is people living together as friends.

And finally, to be fully human is to live in friendship with God.

We know that friendship with other people requires time and sharing; it needs communication and fellowship. This is true also of friendship with God. Think once more of that odd fact that, from the beginning, God has wanted to talk with his creatures. It means God has wanted friendship with us. With two people in the Bible, he seems to have achieved it, the two with whom he talked the most, namely, Abraham and Moses. They talked to God face to face, as one does with a friend. To speak with God was certainly Job's desire, although in his case the desired speaking was more along the lines of speaking (I write this ironically) "man to man" about his grievances. Job's frustration was that he couldn't put God in the dock and question him. Job felt it was unfair. He was wrong, but he was not as wrong as his own friends, who did not think there was anything to talk with God about.

The Bible is odd this way. Its point seems to be that God wants to have real friendship with us, even though that is hard (see Job). In the end, it turns out that to be fully human is to be more than human; it is to be someone that God has taken as a friend.

Behold the man on the cross: behold God's friend.

DISCUSSION QUESTIONS FOR CHAPTER 5

1. What memories do you have of lines you heard or feelings you got from Easter sermons?
2. Have you ever been with someone at the moment of death? What was it like? As you think of Jesus' death, can you imagine their two deaths being united in some way? How? (If you have never been with someone at the time of death, think of a death of someone you knew and what you have been told about it. Can you imagine that death and Jesus' as being in some way together?)
3. The author claims that the point of all God's actions, culminating in Jesus' death and resurrection, is to make friendship possible. Does this claim surprise you? What might God do (or what has God done) to invite you into friendship with him?

Acknowledgments

It was my brave and orthodox bishop, George Sumner, who asked me to think about some basic Christian teaching for our churches as we began to reemerge from the pandemic period. From that nudge came this book. I am grateful to him for calling me to Dallas to be theologian-in-residence and rejoice in our fellowship.

My friends David Daniel and Jonathan Jameson read this manuscript in draft and, as friends should, offered comments both encouraging and incisive. Friends share a common mind, and yet it has surprised me to find they know me in some ways better than I know myself. I thank them even as I beg their forbearance for whatever errors they saw that I have stubbornly failed to correct! If I may add a personal note: one wants one's friends to be friends of each other, and it delights me to note these friends' names, David and Jonathan. (In fact, I think they may be better friends than the biblical David and Jonathan, but that's another sermon for another day.)

The priest who told me of her parishioners who died of COVID (she could have only one conversation with them, and that just by iPad) is Susan Ironside. I am glad to call her a friend and appreciate her permission to retell this story.

To think about God and humanity is, for me, to feel gratitude for and indebtedness to both teachers and students, an almost countless host now stretching across decades, along with numerous theological authors and clerical colleagues. I could name many; let me name two.

When I began doctoral study, Brian Davies opened my mind to basic truths about creation through an extended study of Aquinas's Five Ways for seeing that God exists. That was in 1995. I remember a parishioner early on noting this new turn in my teaching; it changed what I preached and taught, and the last quarter-century has been little more than an effort to think through what was then given. I have also admired Professor Davies's desire to write with simple words, without academic jargon.

From Andrew Mead, who brought me to work with him for a decade at Saint Thomas Church in New York City, I learned not to be afraid of words like doctrine. Father Mead was clear in his mind that the most important thing he did was catechesis. Christian doctrine was infused through his sermons, his classes, and his pastoral care. His spirit, I hope, can be found in this book; however much my style differs from his, my desire is to be in essentials the same: faithful, clear, and bold.

Bibliography

Aquinas, Thomas. *Summa Theologiae*. Summa-Theologiae, n.d. www.summa-theologiae.org.

Aristotle. *Politics*. Translated by Benjamin Jowett. In *The Basic Works of Aristotle*, edited by Richard McKeon, 1113–316. New York: Random House, 1941.

Augustine. *Confessions*. Translated by Henry Chadwick. Oxford, UK: Oxford University Press, 1991.

Austin, Victor Lee. *Friendship: The Heart of Being Human*. Grand Rapids: Baker Academic, 2020.

The Book of Common Prayer. New York: Church Hymnal, 1979.

Capon, Robert Farrar. *The Supper of the Lamb*. New York: Harcourt Brace Jovanovich, 1967.

Dotson, Taylor. "Radiation Politics in a Pandemic." *New Atlantis*, June 18, 2020. https://www.thenewatlantis.com/publications/radiation-politics-in-a-pandemic.

Godwin, Gail. *The Good Husband*. New York: Ballantine, 1994.

Gundry, Robert H. *Matthew: A Commentary on His Handbook for a Mixed Church under Persecution*. 2nd ed. Grand Rapids: Eerdmans, 1994.

Jenson, Robert W. *A Theology in Outline: Can These Bones Live?* Transcribed and edited by Adam Eitel. New York: Oxford University Press, 2016.

Lewis, C. S. *The Great Divorce*. 1946. Reprint, New York: HarperCollins, 2001.

McCabe, Herbert. *God Matters*. 1987. Reprint, London: Continuum, 2005.

Miller, Walter M., Jr. *A Canticle for Leibowitz*. New York: Harper & Row, 1959.

O'Donovan, Oliver. *Begotten or Made?* Oxford, UK: Clarendon, 1984.

———. *The Desire of the Nations*. Cambridge, UK: Cambridge University Press, 1996.

Pope, Alexander. *An Essay on Criticism*. Poetry Foundation, 1711. https://www.poetryfoundation.org/poems/44897/an-essay-on-criticism-part-2.

Sacks, Robert D. *The Lion and the Ass: Reading Genesis after Babylon*. Santa Fe: Kafir Yaroq, 2019.

Whitehead, Alfred North. *Process and Reality*. New York: Macmillan, 1929.

Wright, N. T. *Surprised by Hope*. New York: HarperOne, 2008.

CPSIA information can be obtained
at www.ICGtesting.com
Printed in the USA
LVHW110534041122
732160LV00002B/228